Social Security and the Stock Market

Social Security and the Stock Market

How the Pursuit of Market Magic Shapes the System

Alicia H. Munnell
Steven A. Sass

2006

W.E. Upjohn Institute for Employment Research
Kalamazoo, Michigan

Library of Congress Cataloging-in-Publication Data

Munnell, Alicia Haydock.
  Social security and the stock market : how the pursuit of market magic shapes the system / Alicia H. Munnell Steven A. Sass.
    p. cm.
  ISBN-13: 978-0-88099-290-9 (pbk. : alk. paper)
  ISBN-10: 0-88099-290-5 (pbk. : alk. paper)
  ISBN-13: 978-0-88099-291-6 (hardcover : alk. paper)
  ISBN-10: 0-88099-291-3 (hardcover : alk. paper)
1. Social security—United States—Finance. 2. Pension trusts—Investments—United States. 3. Stock exchanges—United States. 4. Social security—Cross-cultural studies. I. Sass, Steven A., 1949- II. Title.
  HD7125.M755 2006
  368.4'300973—dc22

                                    2006024631

The facts presented in this study and the observations and viewpoints expressed are the sole responsibility of the authors. They do not necessarily represent positions of the W.E. Upjohn Institute for Employment Research.

Cover design by Alcorn Publication Design.
Index prepared by Nancy Humphreys.
Printed in the United States of America.
Printed on recycled paper.

Contents

Boxes

Figures

Tables

Acknowledgments

This book could not have seen the light of day were it not for the help of our friends. Marric Buessing, Luke Delorme, Joel Lieginger, and Kevin Meme, all at the Center for Retirement Research at Boston College, provided excellent research assistance. Andrew Eschtruth and Francis Vitagliano, also at the Center, added astute and careful editing. Marric Buessing also kept our wits, cites, and footnotes in order through the hectic process of preparing the manuscript for publication.

The manuscript benefited from astute comments by Steven Goss, Michael Orszag, John Myles, Daniel Béland, and James Pesando, who read drafts of manuscripts that eventually became chapters of the book. Robert M. Ball, Peter A. Diamond, and H. Allan Hunt read the entire manuscript and greatly improved our presentation and arguments. The Upjohn Institute's anonymous reviewers saved us from error at key junctures and helped clarify our arguments. Robert Wathan thankfully gave our prose a final cleaning, making it far more readable. The Institute's Kevin Hollenbeck and Allison Colosky also kept the editorial and production process moving forward with commendable efficiency.

In addition to providing wonderful editorial and production assistance, we thank the Upjohn Institute for its financial support. We also thank the Alfred P. Sloan Foundation and the Cogan Family Foundation for their support of research that significantly contributed to the arguments and analysis presented in this volume.

1
Introduction

The retirement of the baby boomers will initiate a dramatic aging of the U.S. population. The baby boom, the large generation born between 1946 and 1964, is currently of working age. But the entire generation turns 65, the traditional work-retirement divide, between 2010 and 2030. As the generations that follow are of roughly similar size, a roughly stable labor force will have to support an enormous expansion of the elderly population.

Most elderly people in the United States, defined as the population age 65 and over, currently enjoy a reasonably secure and adequate income. This income comes largely from two main sources—Social Security and employer-sponsored retirement plans. The impending demographic transition, and the rapid decline of employer support for traditional defined-benefit pensions, threatens the nation's ability to provide reasonably secure and adequate old-age incomes going forward.

Reform, however, has been difficult. Policymakers, and people in general, tend to ignore problems lying far in the future, and Social Security has enough money to pay full benefits until 2041. Most people also thought that the growth of 401(k) plans, and similar individual account retirement savings plans, would be able to replace the decline in traditional employer-sponsored pensions. Policymakers did address the problem facing Social Security in the early 1980s by cutting benefits and increasing revenues, but they did not significantly alter the design of the program. By the 1990s, however, deficits reemerged. Concerns also grew over the ability of 401(k)s to replace traditional employer-sponsored pensions. A widening ideological divide and resistance to tax increases, benefit cuts, and government regulation have meanwhile resulted in political deadlock. Interestingly, policymakers of all stripes have embraced the use of investments in equities as an important component of their proposals to reform Social Security, but there is no consensus on how this should be done.[1]

The purpose of this book is to explore the use of equities to help solve the Social Security financing problem. Equities offer a promising way forward due to the high expected returns on stocks and the diversification of the program's funding sources beyond the payroll tax. But the use of equities would also introduce a host of new and difficult challenges and could dramatically change the structure of Social Security in the United States.

To identify the challenges and implications for the structure of the nation's retirement income system, this book explores the experience of the United Kingdom, Australia, and Canada. These three nations initially had retirement income systems quite similar to the U.S. system, in that they relied on both government and employer plans to provide the bulk of old-age income. These countries also face similar demographic and economic challenges. In response, they each introduced equities into their Social Security programs.

The reforms adopted by these nations largely mirror the three proposals that came out of the 1994–1996 Social Security Advisory Council—proposals that define the primary approaches for including equities in the U.S. Social Security program. The United Kingdom introduced equities through a system of "carve-out" individual accounts, whereby Social Security revenues are not increased but a portion can be diverted to individual accounts, where they can be invested in equities. Canada adopted the "trust fund investment" approach, which prefunds future Social Security obligations by building up assets in a trust fund and investing a portion of those assets in equities. Australia adopted a reform similar to the "add-on individual accounts" proposal, although the analogy is somewhat weaker than in the other two cases, where the government mandates contributions to individual accounts that can be invested in equities. The experience of these three nations sheds light on the risks and complications associated with the use of equities in the U.S. Social Security program and how the introduction of equity investment in Social Security could reshape the nation's retirement income system.

Additional information on the challenges created by equity investment also emerges from an analysis of the history of employer-sponsored defined-benefit plans. These plans were once the backbone of the employer-based retirement income system in the United States and these three other nations. They are now in the process of being replaced by 401(k)-type individual account retirement savings plans. Factors contributing to this shift are the risk and uncertainty that equity investment in pension funds create for employers. Identifying the pitfalls that have plagued the private sector provides insights on the ability of public plans to introduce equity investment.

Any change to the nation's Social Security system must be evaluated within the context of the other sources of income available to older people. In the United States, the shift to 401(k) plans means that individuals are exposed to market risk during the accumulation phase and interest rate risk at retirement in their supplementary retirement plans. This exposure increases the desirability of introducing equities into the public plan in a way that minimizes the risk faced by the individual.

WHAT EQUITIES CAN AND CANNOT DO

It is important to clarify that introducing equities into the Social Security program, by itself, will not significantly reduce the burden on future generations of providing for a greatly expanded elderly population. The primary way to reduce that burden is to increase national saving. Without an increase in national saving, the accumulation of equities in the Social Security trust fund, and decumulation of Treasury bonds, would only produce an offsetting reduction in equities held by the general public, and an increase in the public's holdings of Treasury bonds. More saving, on the other hand, means more investment, increased productivity growth, and a bigger economic pie down the road. This bigger pie would ease the burden on future workers, leaving them more national output after they meet the claims of the elderly. To increase national saving, however, the current generation would have to reduce current consumption to increase contributions to the retirement income system or other saving vehicles.

The proposals to reform Social Security that involve equity investment would accumulate these assets either in the Social Security trust fund or in individual accounts. Economists worry, however, that both approaches might be less than fully effective as a mechanism for building national savings. Many economists claim that the accumulation of Treasury bonds in the Social Security trust fund, following the reform of the program in the early 1980s, led to an expansion of government spending that offset the buildup of trust fund reserves and its positive effect on national saving. Shifting trust fund investments from Treasury bonds to stocks would help address this problem, but concerns remain about using the government as a custodian of national savings. Economists are also concerned about the effectiveness of individual accounts as a mechanism for increasing national savings. If workers see their retirement wealth as more immediate and real as a result of this transition, they could be tempted to increase consumption and reduce other forms of saving.

While investment in equities, by itself, does not ease the burden on future generations, it could have two important advantages. The first is an improvement in intergenerational risk sharing (Bohn 1997; Diamond 1997). In general, efficient risk sharing requires individuals to bear more risk when young and less when old. This is because it is easier for the young to work more if they suffer a capital loss. They can also average returns over time and take advantage of the fact that declines in stock prices are typically associated with higher returns in the next period. As the old are in the process of liquidating their equity holdings, they cannot take full advantage of this property. It is also reasonable to assume that the young are less risk averse than the old and hence more inclined to carry stock market risk.

However, the young generally hold no risky, high-yielding assets, and their implicit asset—Social Security—is invested in Treasury bonds. Introducing equities into the Social Security program, either through the trust fund or individual accounts, would shift the portfolio of assets held by the young to include less low-risk, low-return bonds and more high-risk, high-return stocks. If the financial assets in the economy remain unchanged, the portfolios of the old would hold more bonds and less stock. Introducing equities into the Social Security program thus shifts risk from the old to the young, which improves the age distribution of risk and could make all generations better off (Arrow and Lind 1970).

The second argument in favor of equity investment is more political than economic—that it could make Social Security less expensive and diminish pressure to cut benefits or increase taxes. Even without an increase in national saving, introducing equities with their higher expected returns into Social Security should increase the flow of income going to the expanding elderly population. It would give the elderly a larger share of the economic pie and a smaller share to the young. But, rather than accomplishing this transfer through higher payroll taxes, the burden of supporting the expanded elderly population would be met through a reduction in the capital income of young investors, who would hold more bonds and fewer equities than they otherwise would. By making Social Security benefits less expensive, including equity investments would thus reduce political risk to the program.

EVALUATING EQUITY RISKS IN RETIREMENT PLANS

A central issue in the debate over the introduction of equities is the thorny question of how to treat the risk in such investments when evaluating the finances of retirement income systems. Some experts argue that holding equities should reduce the projected contributions required to fund a defined-benefit plan, such as Social Security, or increase the projected income generated in individual retirement accounts. After all, stocks yield 7 percent after inflation and bonds only 3 percent. Others claim this is nonsense. The higher expected return on equities reflects their greater risk. Any serious financial evaluation of retirement arrangements, they say, must "risk-adjust" these returns. After accounting for risk, the amount of contributions needed to fund future pension obligations (or the amount of income an individual account could generate) is the same regardless of whether the assets are invested in equities or bonds.

There is no clear consensus within the government on how to evaluate the use of equities in Social Security reform proposals. The Social Security actuaries take the first approach and credit equities with their expected rate of return. The Congressional Budget Office (CBO), a key government gatekeeper, ignores the higher expected return and credits equities as yielding the long-term Treasury rate. The CBO, in effect, views the cost of the additional risk in stocks as precisely offsetting their additional return.

The government also confronted this issue when Congress introduced equities into the funding of the Railroad Retirement System in 2001. Congress raised benefits, reduced contributions, and sought to square the circle by authorizing investments in equities and other non-traditional assets. But the Office of Management and Budget (OMB), another key government scoring agency, ignored the higher expected return on equities and used the long-term Treasury rate to project future trust fund balances. Like the CBO, the OMB viewed the additional risk in stocks as precisely offsetting the additional return.[2] The agency clearly sought to avoid a situation where the government could appear to raise money simply by issuing debt and buying stock with the proceeds.

Adjusting for risk makes an enormous difference when assessing Social Security reform proposals that rely on equity investments. Projections using the riskless rate produce no reduction in the funding shortfall in trust fund investment proposals and dramatic benefit reductions in carve-out individual account proposals.[3]

What then is the best way to evaluate the use of equities in retirement plans? It depends on the objective.

If the goal is to compare different proposals with the current system for policy purposes, then the bond return is the appropriate choice. The only way to get an "apples-to-apples" comparison is to look at streams of income with similar risk characteristics, and bonds rather than equities have the characteristics most similar to benefits under the current system.

If the goal is to assess the likely outcome under a reformed system, the evaluation is more complex. The natural instinct is to think that investing in equities will *probably* lead to a higher benefit in individual account proposals (or smaller deficits in the trust fund investment proposals) since equities have historically outperformed bonds. The extent to which individual participants (or future taxpayers) can capture these higher returns, however, depends on their ability to manage the risk. If participants (or taxpayers) have other resources or can pool risk or delay retirement, they could weather market downturns more easily. Or, if the risks are pooled across individuals and over generations by having the trust fund invest in equities, they can be managed more efficiently. These risk management considerations have a direct impact on the ability of different reform proposals to capture the higher expected return on equities, after properly subtracting the cost of the risk in such investments.

The different approaches to introducing equities into the Social Security program, in other words, are far from equal. The distribution of risk and its implications, as well as more conventional costs and benefits, depend crucially on whether equities enter the program through individual accounts or the Social Security trust fund. Transaction costs and governance challenges—many of which emerge in response to the risk in equity investment—also vary dramatically from one approach to another.

THE OUTLOOK FOR THE U.S. RETIREMENT SYSTEM

The majority of the elderly currently enjoy a relatively good economic position. Their cash incomes are generally lower than what they earned prior to retirement, but they need less. They no longer pay Social Security payroll taxes and typically pay less income tax. Their children are typically out of the house and no longer a drain on their incomes. Nor do they have working expenses. The elderly typically own their homes free and clear and do not have to save for retirement. The freedom from having to work, and the ability to use one's time to shop more effectively, produce goods and services previously purchased on the market, and generally enjoy life as one sees fit, are important lifestyle advantages. All in all, the elderly generally enjoy a standard of living not much different from that of their preretirement years.

The retirement income of the elderly comes from two main sources—Social Security and employer retirement plans. As Figure 1.1 shows, Social Security alone supplies 37 percent of the income of the elderly, 52 percent if earnings from work are excluded. Employer-sponsored retirement plans provide another 20 percent, over a quarter when earnings from work are excluded, and are especially important for middle- and upper-middle-income households. The only other significant sources of old-age income—investment income and earnings from work—are important only for those at the top of the income scale, and earnings from work, which tend to put recipients in the upper quintile, disappear as individuals age.

However, Social Security and employer plans are ill-equipped to provide the same level of support going forward. Legislation enacted in 1983, which raised the "normal retirement age" from 65 to 67 between 2000 and 2022, has already resulted in cuts in the level of preretirement earnings that Social Security will replace, and rising health care costs will dramatically eat into future Social Security payments.[4]

Figure 1.1 Retirement Income by Source in the United States, 2004

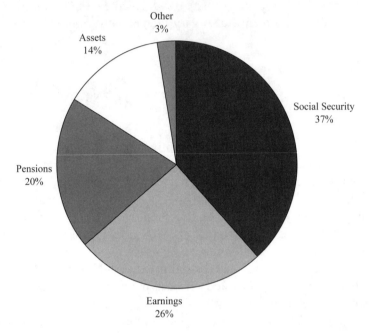

SOURCE: Author's calculations based on U.S. Census Bureau, 2005 Current Population Survey.

Major changes in the nature of employer plans raise critical questions as to their ability to replace the same share of earnings in the future as they currently do, let alone make up for the decline in Social Security. Americans thus face the prospect of a sharp drop in their standard of living in retirement, with the fall-off getting steeper with each succeeding cohort.

The Future of Social Security

Under Social Security, active workers pay into the program, and they or their families receive benefits when they retire, become disabled, or die. The system functions on a partially funded basis. Roughly 75 percent of current revenues go to pay current benefits, and the remainder is used to build up the Social Security trust fund. Over the next

75 years, benefit costs will rise as the population ages. The ratio of the elderly population (age 65 or over) to working age adults (ages 20–64) will rise from 20 percent today to about 35 percent by 2030 (Figure 1.2). The child dependency ratio—the ratio of the population age 19 or younger to working-age adults—will decline, offsetting some of the rising aged dependency burden. Because the elderly consume far more resources per capita than children, the offset is not one for one.

The rise in the number of elderly relative to the working-age population will increase the cost of Social Security benefits well above payroll tax receipts (Figure 1.3). Without any change, future revenues combined with the assets in the trust fund will allow Social Security to pay 100 percent of benefits until 2040. Once the trust fund is exhausted, revenues will cover only about 70 percent of scheduled benefits. The federal budget will be affected earlier, when Social Security begins to redeem its trust fund assets. Instead of being a steady purchaser of government bonds, Social Security will become an added burden on the Treasury's fund-raising operations.

Figure 1.2 U.S. Population Age 65+ as a Percentage of Population 20–64, 1950–2050

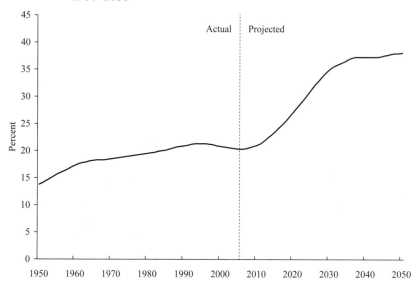

SOURCE: U.S. Social Security Administration (2006).

Figure 1.3 Projected U.S. Social Security Revenue and Benefit Rates as a Percent of Covered Payroll, 2004–2080

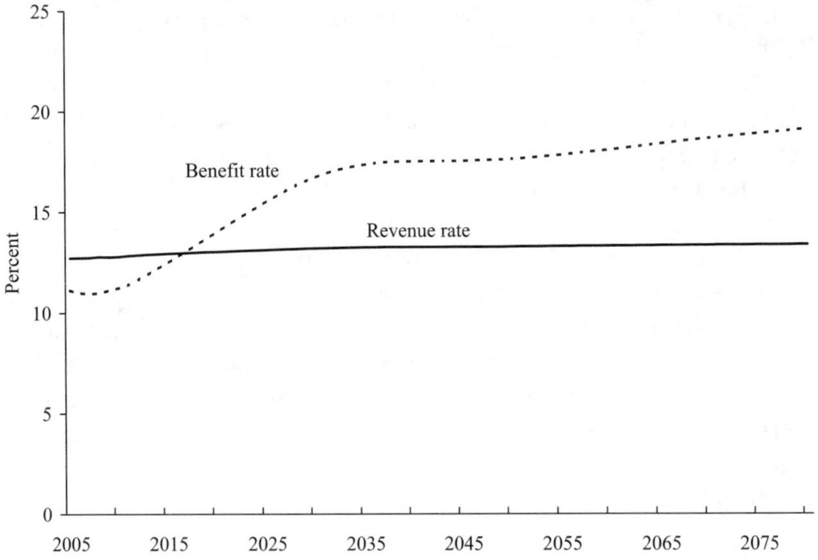

SOURCE: U.S. Social Security Administration (2006).

Each year, the Office of the Actuary of Social Security prepares a high, low, and intermediate cost projection for the financial position of the program for the following 75 years, with the intermediate projection playing a central role in the political process. In 2006, the difference over the projection period between the present discounted value of promised benefits and the present discounted value of projected revenues, using the intermediate cost estimate, was $4.9 trillion (Table 1.1). Since the economy is projected to grow tremendously over the 75-year period, the dollar deficit is usually expressed as a percent of taxable payrolls or gross domestic product (GDP). In 2006, Social Security's 75-year deficit stood at 2.02 percent of taxable payrolls. This figure means that the payroll tax rate needs to be raised immediately by roughly 2 percent of covered earnings—1 percent each for employers and employees—for Social Security to pay the current package of benefits to everyone who reaches retirement age through 2080.

Social Security's long-term financing problem is somewhat more complicated. If balance were restored only over the next 75 years, the

Table 1.1 U.S. Social Security's Financing Shortfall

Period	Present discounted value (trillion $)	As a percent of	
		Taxable payrolls	GDP
2006–2080	4.9[a]	2.02	0.7
2006–Infinity	13.4	3.7	1.3

[a] The $4.9 trillion includes $4.6 trillion, the difference between scheduled benefits and projected revenues, and $343 billion required to bring the trust fund to 100 percent of annual cost by the end of the period.
SOURCE: U.S. Social Security Administration (2006).

system faces a big deficit in the 76th year as the cost of benefits continues to exceed the system's revenues. To avoid this type of financial "cliff," most policymakers support additional revenues or benefit cuts, beyond those needed to restore solvency over Social Security's 75-year planning horizon. Some observers even advocate looking at the deficit over an infinite horizon, which brings the shortfall to 3.7 as a percent of taxable payrolls.

Regardless of how the shortfall is measured, changes are needed to bring Social Security's inflows and outflows back into line. These changes can take the form of benefit cuts, tax increases, or an increase in the returns on assets. As discussed above, many policymakers want to avoid higher taxes or lower benefits and thus have turned to equities as part of the solution.

Policymakers are reluctant to cut benefits because Social Security is already scheduled to replace a significantly smaller portion of preretirement earnings than it does today. A person with average earnings retiring at 65 currently receives benefits equal to $1,180 per month or about 42 percent of previous earnings. After the Medicare Part B premium is automatically deducted from Social Security benefits, the replacement rate drops to 38.5 percent. Under *current law,* Social Security replacement rates—benefits as a percent of preretirement earnings—are scheduled to decline at any given retirement age for three reasons. First, the increase in the normal retirement age from 65 to 67, currently in progress, is equivalent to an across-the-board cut. Second, Medicare Part B premiums are slated to increase sharply due to rising health care costs. Finally, Social Security benefits will be taxed more under the personal income tax, as the exemption amounts are not indexed to inflation. As shown in Table 1.2, these three factors will reduce the net replacement

Table 1.2 U.S. Social Security Replacement Rates for Average Earner Retiring at Age 65, 2005 and 2030

Provision	Replacement rate (%)
2005	
Reported replacement rate	42.2
After Medicare Part B deduction	38.5
2030	
Replacement rate after extension of normal retirement age	36.3
After deduction for Medicare Part B	32.0
After personal income taxation	29.3

SOURCE: Munnell (2003) and authors' updates.

rate for the average earner who retires at age 65 from 38.5 percent today to 29.3 percent in 2030, or $800 in today's terms. Restoring solvency through cuts in benefits would reduce this level of support still further.

The Future of Employer-Sponsored Retirement Plans

Employer-sponsored retirement plans, the only other important source of income for most older Americans, seem ill-equipped to fill in the gap. Indeed, most observers question their ability to provide the same level of replacement income that they do today. The problem is not that a smaller share of the workforce participates in an employer plan. Participation rates have been remarkably steady over the past quarter century, at about half the private sector workforce, and they are likely to remain much the same going forward. Rather, the nature of these plans has changed so dramatically that it is very difficult to predict the income they will provide when the baby boom retires.

As noted above, employer plans currently provide 20 percent of the cash income of individuals age 65 and over—27 percent if we exclude earnings from work. For those retiring today, this income comes primarily from traditional "defined-benefit" pension plans. These plans typically pay benefits based on a combination of the worker's final salary and years of service with the employer. The actual benefits workers get in retirement vary quite a bit, depending on how often they changed jobs. Once a worker retires, these pensions generally remain the same until the worker dies. The major uncertainty is the rate of inflation because benefits are generally defined as a fixed dollar amount and lose purchasing power as prices rise. The elderly nevertheless can rely on a reasonably secure stream of income for the remainder of their lives.

Most baby boomers, by contrast, are covered by "defined-contribution" plans (Figure 1.4). In these arrangements, workers and their employers contribute a defined portion of the worker's wage to an individual savings account. At retirement, the worker gets the accumulated contributions and investment income as a lump sum. The retirement income these plans provide depends on a host of factors, including how much workers and employers contribute, the real after-inflation return on assets in the accounts, how workers draw down their balances (both before and after retirement), and how long they live. Given the experience to date, defined contribution plans are unlikely to replace a greater share of preretirement income than defined-benefit plans. This income

Figure 1.4 Coverage by Type of Plan, U.S. Private Sector Wage and Salary Workers with Pension Coverage, 1981–2004

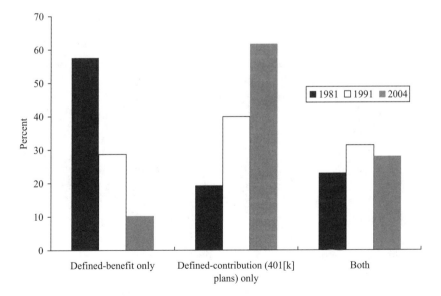

SOURCE: Buessing and Soto (2006).

is also subject to significantly greater risks and uncertainties than a traditional pension. As a result, employer-sponsored plans in the future are unlikely to be as secure and reliable a source of retirement income as they are today. The baby boom generation thus faces the prospect of a sharp decline in living standards at retirement and even serious hardship as they age (see Box 1.1).

The challenge is to restore solvency to the Social Security program, make employer-sponsored plans work as well as they can, and maintain the contribution of these programs to retirement income security.[5] As noted above, many proposals to eliminate Social Security's financing shortfall involve the introduction of equities in one form or another. The following chapters review the creation of modern retirement income systems, examine the current situation in the United States and the experience of reforms enacted in the United Kingdom, Australia, and Canada, and draw lessons for the United States on how the introduction of equity investments into the Social Security program could affect individuals and influence the evolution of the nation's retirement income system.

Box 1.1 It's Not Just the Baby Boom

The American population has been aging ever since the founding of the republic, the result primarily of declining fertility and rising life expectancy. Over the 200-year period between 1880 and 2080, the shape of the U.S. age distribution will change from a pyramid to almost a rectangle as the relative number of older people rises and the relative number of children declines (see the adjoining figure). Note that neither date that brackets this 200-year period has anything to do with the baby boom generation; 1880 predates the first boomer by more than six decades, and by 2080 virtually all the boomers will have died. (The youngest boomers, born in 1964, would be 116 years old in 2080.) The passage of the baby boom affects the timing of population aging, but the phenomenon is the result of the long decline in the number of babies per woman and of the increase in life expectancy.

Box 1.1 (continued)

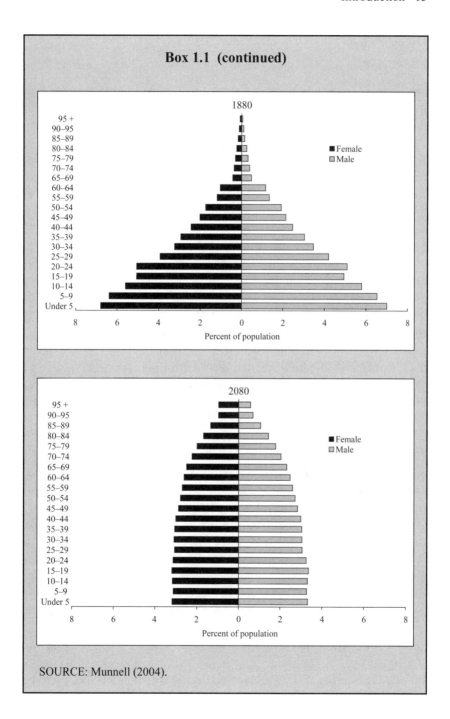

SOURCE: Munnell (2004).

ORGANIZATION OF THE VOLUME

Chapter 2 describes how retirement income systems emerged in all industrial nations in response to a common set of problems. These nations now all face the challenge of rapid population aging, and three countries that had a mix of government and employer plans much like ours (the United Kingdom, Australia, and Canada) have responded with reforms incorporating equity investment that are especially instructive for the United States. Most nations on the European continent, by contrast, opted for public or publicly directed solutions. The experience of other Anglo-Saxon nations is thus most relevant to policymakers in the United States.

Chapter 3 describes the challenges facing the U.S. retirement income system. After 1980, serious solvency problems emerged in both employer defined-benefit pension plans and Social Security. Reforms addressing the solvency of employer plans have been relatively ineffective, largely due to their inability to address the risk in equity investments. A far more important change in employer plans has been the shift from defined-benefit to defined-contribution formats—a change that exacerbated the risks in private retirement income programs, reduced the ability to effectively manage such programs, and raised new questions about retirement income adequacy.

A major reform of the Social Security program, in 1983, cut benefits, increased contributions, and restored solvency over the program's 75-year planning horizon. The funding shortfall reemerged, however, as the passage of time brought more years on the other side of the funding "cliff" within the program's 75-year planning horizon.

The 1994–1996 Social Security Advisory Council attempted to fix the problem. The council members resisted—for different reasons—restoring balance simply by raising taxes or cutting benefits. They all resorted to a new source of revenue—namely, the higher expected return on equity investment—but failed to reach a consensus around a single plan. Instead, the council produced three separate proposals: 1) "carve out" individual accounts invested in equities, funded by redirecting a significant portion of current payroll taxes and sharply reducing the guaranteed social insurance benefit; 2) "add-on" individual accounts, invested in equities, that would top up the reduced benefits that could be financed by the payroll tax; and 3) a portion of trust fund assets invested in equities. No action has since been taken, and these three options remain on the table. The United Kingdom, Australia, and Canada have all introduced equities into their Social Security programs, each along the lines of one of these three approaches.

Chapter 4 reviews the experience of the United Kingdom, which reformed its retirement income system and introduced equities along the lines of the carve-out approach. To achieve solvency, the government sharply cut traditional social insurance benefits. To raise retirement incomes back toward levels initially envisioned for the public program, it allowed workers to carve out a portion of their payroll tax to contribute to an individual account that invests in equities. In exchange, workers give up a portion of their diminished Social Security benefits.

The British experience clearly illustrates a series of shortcomings to such an approach. Individual accounts, which were primarily offered in the financial marketplace rather than through an employer- or government-run program, encountered high administrative costs that market forces have not been able to reduce. Major scandals also illustrate serious difficulties in protecting unsophisticated workers from misleading selling practices. Meanwhile, the government's guaranteed social security benefits have fallen below the traditional income floor guaranteed by the public welfare system—20 percent of national average earnings. In response, the government expanded the means-tested benefits for the elderly. To mitigate the disincentive to work or save created by these means-tested benefits, Britain introduced a tapered withdrawal rate for the elderly—reducing means-tested benefits by 40 pence per pound, rather than pound for pound. As a result, half the elderly are now eligible for welfare benefits and three-quarters are projected to be eligible by the middle of the century.

Proponents of the carve-out approach generally claim that they want to reduce dependence on the state and increase reliance on individual initiative and private financial markets. The British experience suggests that the outcome of the carve-out approach is likely to be a major expansion in means-tested benefits, just the opposite of the desired increase in self-reliance.

Chapter 5 reviews the experience of Australia, which reformed its system and introduced equities along the lines of the add-on approach. The analogy is not perfect, but the introduction of individual accounts was accompanied by a big increase in contributions. Australia added mandatory contributions to individual retirement savings accounts, which could invest in equities, atop its preexisting public pension program. In Australia, these mandatory contributions are generally collected and invested collectively, which reduces administrative costs and relieves workers of many of the decisions they have to make in the UK system. The other component of Australia's retirement income system is its means-tested Age Pension. The Age Pension is far more generous than the UK means-tested program; it guarantees an income of about a third of national average earnings, reduced by 40 cents for each dollar of other income above a minimal amount. Nearly all elderly Australians qualify for a full or partial benefit. In a system dependent on individual accounts invested in equities, the Age Pension means test performs a valuable risk-management service. It assures a reasonably comfortable income to those who outlive their individual account assets, invest poorly, or are in unlucky cohorts when it comes to investment returns. The Age Pension, however, also creates a powerful disincentive to work or save that should become a serious problem as assets build up in the nation's mandatory savings program.

Chapter 6 reviews the experience of Canada, which reformed its system and introduced equities along the lines of the trust fund approach. It accelerated scheduled tax increases to prefund future benefits (which the United States had done in 1983) and invested the accumulated assets in equities (whereas the United States stayed with government bonds). The trust fund approach has significant financial advantages over the use of individual accounts, especially if the policy objective is to achieve some specified level of retirement income. It is much better at handling the risks inherent in equity investment and avoids the work and saving disincentives seen in the Australian system. The trust fund approach also has much lower administrative and governance costs. The power it potentially puts in the hands of government, however, raises serious political issues. In response, Canada developed an elaborate governance design to minimize political involvement in the management of trust fund assets. Although the program has only been in place a few years, the Canadian experience suggests that the problem is manageable. It also appears considerably less daunting than the task of governing equity investments in a myriad of Social Security individual accounts.

Chapter 7 reviews the lessons drawn from the foreign experience. It suggests that the trust fund approach, adopted by Canada, may be the most promising way to introduce equities into the U.S. Social Security program. Although the program is relatively new, trust fund investment in equities seems like the most efficient way to manage the risks and administrative challenges inherent in equity investment while delivering a targeted level of retirement income. The Canadians have also developed a governance system that illustrates the ability of government to keep investment management essentially free of political influence. The Canadian approach seems to be well regarded both in Canada and internationally. Holding equities in add-on individual accounts, the approach adopted by Australia, also bears consideration. It adds significant resources to the system and increases national saving. Holding equities in individual accounts carved out of the Social Security program, the approach adopted by the United Kingdom, is clearly problematic. The British experiment shows how this approach precipitated the conversion of the UK retirement income system into a combination of large and risky individual accounts atop a minimal means-tested welfare program, with most of the nation's elderly at some point in their lives dependent on means-tested welfare benefits.

Notes

1. Not all proposals to restore solvency to the Social Security program involve equity investment. See Diamond and Orszag (2004) and Smetters (1997).
2. The Office of Management and Budget (OMB) provides a full discussion of the need to risk-adjust expected returns: "Equities and private bonds earn a higher return on average than the Treasury rate, but that return is subject to greater uncertainty. Sound budget principles require that estimates of future trust fund balances reflect both the average return and cost of risk associated with the uncertainty of that return. . . . Economic theory suggests, however, that the difference between the expected return of a risky liquid asset and the Treasury rate is equal to the cost of the asset's additional risk as priced in the market. Following through on this insight, the best way to project the rate of return on the fund's balances is to use the Treasury rate" (OMB 2003).

   Most economists seem to agree on the need to risk-adjust returns when evaluating Social Security reform proposals. Geanakoplos, Mitchell, and Zeldes (2002) note that "our view is that the risk-adjusted NPV [net present value] measure is most helpful for ranking alternative" proposals. More recently, Diamond and Orszag (2004) use risk-adjusted returns to evaluate proposals that include individual accounts. Others, however, continue to embrace the "best-guess" actuarial approach (Biggs 2002).

3. Option pricing techniques can also be used to calculate the risk-reward trade-offs. See Bodie (2001).

4. The normal retirement age will rise from 65, for those reaching age 62 prior to the year 2000, to age 67 for those who reach 62 in 2022 or after.

5. For a discussion of proposals to reform current 401(k) plans, see Munnell and Sundén (2004).

2

The Creation of Modern
Retirement Income Systems

The elderly in modern industrial economies get the bulk of their income from two main sources—government old-age pensions and government subsidized and regulated employer-based plans. This is strikingly new. Prior to 1900, retirement itself was rare. Only as the twentieth century progressed did public and employer pensions come to support the elderly population in industrial economies. And only in the past generation did they come to eclipse all other sources of income and allow the elderly to maintain a reasonable approximation of their preretirement standard of living.

Retirement income systems in industrialized countries evolved in two very different ways after the Second World War. The nations on the European continent, with private industry devastated by the war and with stronger traditions of publicly provided welfare, opted for systems of generous government-provided pensions.[1] These programs came to replace 60 percent or more of a worker's preretirement earnings. In the United States and other "Anglo-Saxon" nations, such as the United Kingdom, Australia, and Canada, employers were spared the worst ravages of war and conservative political parties had a far more restrictive view of the role of the state. These countries maintained a mixed public-employer system. This chapter describes the evolution of these retirement income systems, focusing primarily on developments in Anglo-Saxon nations similar to the United States, to gain a better understanding of the rationale and structure of such systems and the challenges they face going forward.

INDUSTRIALIZATION AND THE PROBLEM OF
OLD-AGE INCOMES

In preindustrial economies, the elderly generally continued to work for as long as they could. They took on less taxing jobs as their strength or acuity declined, and stopped working only when no longer able. A 1570 census of the poor in Norwich, England, thus described three widows, ages 74, 79, and 82, as "almost past work" but still earning a small income from spinning. In colonial America, estates left by elderly decedents often included tools used in less strenuous trades, such as tailoring, shoemaking, and weaving. Three of four elderly Americans still worked well into the nineteenth century (Achenbaum 1978; Pelling 1991; Sass 1997; Thane 2000).

The elderly in preindustrial economies also often owned property that provided an income. Family farms and handicraft businesses were natural vehicles for accumulating wealth as part of a worker's normal routine. Through the first half of the nineteenth century, improving family farms was actually the largest component of U.S. capital formation, and many elderly farmers were able to retire from active labor by selling or leasing these assets (Sass 1997; Thane 2000; U.S. Bureau of the Census 1960). The minority of the elderly who could no longer work and had little or no property would often rely on their children for economic support.

What transformed the economics of aging in the nineteenth century were industrialization and the closely related process of urbanization. Industrialization involved the transfer of production from the household to larger and more rationally organized enterprises. Urbanization concentrated the population in the large labor and product markets, which was necessary for the emergence of mass-production mass-distribution enterprises and firms that supplied an increasingly broad array of specialized goods and services. The outcome was an enormously productive economy. Per capita incomes in today's industrialized nations are approximately 15 to 20 times higher than they were in 1820, when the process could be said to have begun (Maddison 1995). As industrialization came to dominate economic production, from the end of the nineteenth and into the twentieth century, it undermined the ability of the elderly to support themselves through work or ownership of income-producing assets. Urbanization also undermined traditional sources of communal assistance.

Workers in industrial economies gain their livelihoods primarily by working for large employers, earning wage and salary incomes, which they use to purchase market-supplied goods and services. But, as workers age, their ability to generate earnings grows increasingly uncertain.

Industrial enterprises are fairly intolerant of an aging worker's declining capabilities. They need to cover the fixed costs of plant, equipment, and supervision just to break even. To maximize profits, they need to operate at a rationally determined pace of production. Even if a worker's labor remained valuable to such employers at age 50 or 60, it rarely would remain so at age 70 or 80 (Margo 1991).

Workers in industrial economies also did not naturally acquire assets that could provide an old-age income. They had no ownership interest in their workplace, as they had in family farms and handicraft businesses. The process of gaining a livelihood was now sharply divorced from the process of acquiring income-producing property. To build up such assets, industrial workers had to consciously set aside a portion of their earnings and use those funds to purchase income-producing property. This saving and investing process required a good deal of foresight, discipline, and skill. It also required a significant aversion to risk. As late as the first decade of the twentieth century, nearly two-thirds of all Americans who reached age 10, and thus had survived childhood diseases, could expect to die before reaching age 70. Given the difficulty in acquiring income-producing assets and the low likelihood of becoming too old to work, it is not surprising that less than half of the Massachusetts elderly in 1910 had *any* income from savings that could offset a decline or cessation of earnings (Sass 1997; Seager 1910; Squirer 1912). As wage and salary earnings tended to vanish as workers aged, industrialization had created a crisis in old-age incomes.

THE EMERGENCE OF NATIONAL RETIREMENT INCOME SYSTEMS: ca. 1850–1940

The response in every industrial nation was the creation of retirement income programs by large employers and national governments—the two institutions that became dramatically more important in modern industrial economies. The earliest programs were pension plans set up by large employers: first governments, then railroads and public utilities, and then large manufacturers and service-providing enterprises. Germany created the first national old-age income program in 1889, and by the end of the 1930s, essentially all industrial nations had such a program.

The Emergence of Employer Pensions

The nineteenth century saw the emergence of a handful of very large employers, such as governments, railroads, utilities, universities, and business corporations, that sought to develop employment relationships with their workers and made the promise of an old-age pension a valuable instrument of personnel management.[2] The first such relationship involved the development of career civil servants and managers.[3] The large, dispersed organizations that emerged in the nineteenth century delegated significant authority to this special class of workers. These workers had to invest in organization-specific skills and relationships, make decisions and execute responsibilities in the best interest of the organization, and do so with limited oversight over their entire working lives. The British civil service pension plan of 1859 became the model for developing such a career managerial workforce in both government and private settings.[4]

Pensions also proved valuable in developing employment relationships with blue-collar workers. Railroad, urban transit, and manufacturing firms employed large numbers of blue-collar workers to operate their capital-intensive, high-throughput operations. In a bid to attract better workers, win their loyalty, and fend off unions, these employers already paid above-market wages. Beyond a certain point, providing "industrial insurance" helped achieve these objectives better than paying ever higher wages. In exchange for the financial stability this insurance provided, employers expected loyalty and diligent service. Unions and workmen's friendly societies also offered such protection, so these employer plans fended off competing claims to their workers' allegiance. Employers could also expect this compensation package to attract workers with a greater sense of responsibility and foresight (Ackerloff 1982; Ippolito 1998; Sass 1997).

Toward the end of the nineteenth century, the opposite problem became the concern of many large employers. Their offices, machine shops, and locomotives were increasingly staffed by older workers whose productive abilities had clearly declined. So, beginning in the 1890s in Britain and at the turn of the century in the United States, large employers began to introduce mandatory retirement at a specified age. To remove these workers without damaging the firm's relationship with the rest of the workforce and the public at large, they retired these workers on pension. Because employers wanted no employee interference in this mandatory retirement policy, they did not require employee contributions. As companies with preexisting pension plans saw the number of older employees steadily rise, many introduced compulsory retirement and likewise assumed the full cost of the plan (Graebner 1980; Lazear 1979; Sass 1997).

By the end of the 1930s, employer plans had become standard in governments and mature big businesses throughout the industrial world; nevertheless, they covered only up to 15 percent of the workforce in industrialized nations such as the United Kingdom, the United States, Australia, and Canada. Many of those covered would also leave their employers prior to retirement, voluntarily or not, and fail to qualify for an old-age pension. Employer plans were thus a personnel policy tool, not the solution to the old-age income problem (Commonwealth Treasury 2001; Coward 1995; Hannah 1986; Sass 1997).

The Emergence of Government Pensions

Toward the end of the nineteenth century, a steadily rising population of elderly poor created increasing pressure for national old-age income programs. National governments responded in one of two ways. Most early initiatives were means-tested programs that took on a portion of the welfare burden from overstressed local communities. Many even used local governments to administer the program. The second approach, social insurance, mirrored the blue-collar industrial insurance programs set up by large employers. Social insurance programs initially targeted the industrial sector and excluded agrarian, self-employed, and white-collar workers. They also protected workers and their families against the loss of those earnings due to death, sickness, disability, unemployment, or age, and typically mandated employee and/or employer contributions that were proportional to earnings.

National means-tested pensions for the elderly were first introduced by small nations with modest industrial sectors: Denmark in 1891, New Zealand in 1898, and the British colony of Victoria (Australia) in 1900 (Table 2.1). Then France introduced means-tested programs in 1907, as did the United Kingdom in 1908. All paid meager benefits and had stringent income and residency tests.[5] Early means-tested plans also required "good character," which generally meant no record of serious

**Table 2.1 The Creation of National Old-Age Pension Programs in
Countries around the World**

Decade	Nations creating means-tested programs	Nations creating social insurance programs
1880s		Germany
1890s	Denmark, New Zealand	
1900s	France, Australia, United Kingdom, Irish Free State, Iceland	
1910s	Newfoundland, Uruguay	France, Luxembourg, Romania, Netherlands, Sweden, Italy, Portugal, Spain
1920s	Norway, Greenland, Canada, South Africa	Greece, Union of Soviet Socialist Republics, Yugoslavia, Belgium, Chile, Czechoslovakia, United Kingdom, Austria, Hungary
1930s		Poland, United States

SOURCE: U.S. Social Security Board (1937).

crime, drunkenness, or other moral failing, no recent application for pauper relief, and 20 or more years of residence.

The German plan of 1889, the first national old-age income program, adopted the social insurance approach. Like the employer blue-collar plans, the German old-age pension was part of a larger initiative that protected industrial workers against a loss of earnings due to illness (in 1883), accidents (in 1884), and then old-age and disability (in 1889). These social insurance programs required weekly contributions that were proportional to earnings and split between workers and employers. The programs also relied on contributions from general government revenues. At age 70, workers were entitled to a pension proportional to their average wage times the number of years in the plan. Even with a full career's contributions, however, this pension replaced only a small portion of preretirement earnings.

The German experiment was not soon repeated. Social insurance was a new and expensive public program. Unlike traditional means-tested assistance, it paid benefits to those who had sufficient resources on their own. It also required a level of compulsion and bureaucratic management that exceeded the capacity of most nineteenth-century states (Massachusetts Commission on Old-Age Pensions 1909; Seager 1910).

After 1910, social insurance became the dominant approach to the old-age income problem. Three out of four national programs enacted after that date adopted the social insurance model. They mandated contributions in the form of a tax on earnings, provided pensions as a matter of right from a specified age, and based benefits on the worker's contribution record. These programs were far from universal. White-collar, agrarian, and self-employed workers were typically excluded. By 1933, however, 20 nations relied on social insurance as their primary old-age income program. Only 12 used means-tested programs.

The United States was late to develop a public old-age pension program. This is explained partly by the sheer size of the nation, encompassing both the industrialized North and the agrarian South and West, and partly by the limited authority of the national government. Politically weak immigrants and their children, moreover, accounted for two-thirds of the blue-collar industrial workforce. The most politically important group in the nation—native-born Northerners—also benefited from a generous pension program for Union Army veterans through the early years of the twentieth century (Sass 1997).

The United States finally created its Social Security program in 1935, in the midst of the Great Depression. The severe economic downturn, combined with a surge in the supply of older workers, dramatically worsened the employment and income problems of the elderly. A critical need for financial support thus emerged at a political moment especially conducive to major institutional innovation. Some experts also contend that the desire to remove older workers from the labor force was another motivating factor. The program enacted in 1935 addressed the immediate crisis with a means-tested program called Old-Age Assistance. It also addressed the continuing problem—providing income for the elderly who could no longer work or find employment—with a social insurance program called Old-Age Benefits. The Old-Age Benefits program is what we now think of as Social Security.

THE ARRIVAL OF "RETIREMENT"

In the period after the Second World War, the economics of the elderly changed dramatically. Essentially all industrial nations now provided old-age pensions, typically at age 65 for men and often earlier for women, which guaranteed a minimal old-age income without the need to work. Government had thus assumed the "industrial insurance" function seen in blue-collar employer plans, essentially providing basic retirement benefits on a universal basis. Public and employer plans also actively encouraged older workers to withdraw from the labor force. Many employers had a mandatory retirement policy. Most public plans had an earnings test that denied benefits to anyone who earned more than a trivial sum.[6] Public and private programs also encouraged retirement by not increasing benefits beyond the normal retirement age. This effectively cut a worker's compensation for remaining employed to the worker's wage less the foregone pension. The combination of a basic old-age income and these incentives to retire reinforced the ongoing decline in the percentage of the elderly who remained in the labor force (Figure 2.1). As longevity was also rising rapidly, retirement soon emerged as an expected, extended, and well-defined stage of life.

The elderly nevertheless remained a distinctly poor population. In Britain, old-age incomes in 1950 averaged only about 40 percent of the average male wage. In the United States, over one-third of the elderly in 1959 were poor. The three decades following the Second World War, however, were a period of unprecedented economic growth. The financial standing of the elderly thus stood in increasingly sharp contrast to the rising prosperity of most working-age adults. A consensus gradually emerged that the elderly should share in this prosperity and that income should be spread more evenly across the lifespan—that active workers should be able to maintain a reasonable approximation of their preretirement standard of living when they in turn grow old.[7] The question was how.

Nations on the European continent opted for a government-directed solution. The Depression and Second World War had destroyed much of the savings of individual workers, the net worth of private employers, and the value of assets held in employer pension funds or by annuity providers. Only government pay-as-you-go transfers, or similar ar-

**Figure 2.1 Percent of People Age 65+ in the Labor Force in the United
States and United Kingdom, 1880–2005**

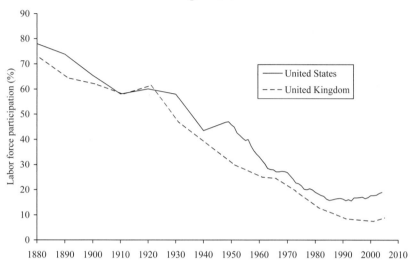

SOURCE: Employment by age based on Bureau of Labor Statistics (2005); Costa (1998);
Moen (1987); UK Office for National Statistics' Labour Force Survey (2005).

rangements mandated and regulated by the government, could quickly
increase the incomes of the elderly. These continental nations had comparatively strong traditions of publicly provided welfare and negotiated
labor-market institutions, deriving variously from autocratic, Catholic
social welfare, or social democratic political traditions. Many countries also institutionalized national wage bargaining after the war, with
the outcomes legally enforceable. These negotiations became the platform for establishing quasi-public mandatory social insurance arrangements that would cover essentially all workers (Esping-Anderson 1990;
Whiteside 2002).

These continental programs—termed "Bismarckian" because benefits were closely tied to earnings and contributions, as in Chancellor
Bismarck's 1889 German program—were substantially expanded in
the second decade following the end of the Second World War. Pensions provided by the state and/or quasi-mandated negotiated arrangements came to replace 60 percent or more of preretirement earnings.
This amount was generally enough to maintain preretirement living

standards with little or no supplementation. (The importance of these programs even today is shown in Figure 2.3 towards the end of this chapter.) Only workers with low incomes or patchy employment histories would need supplementary public support. Households who entered retirement owning their home outright or with some financial assets could actually see their living standards rise. Except for highly paid corporate and government officials, this expansion of public or publicly supervised old-age pensions effectively eliminated the need for employer plans or individual retirement savings.

The United States and other Anglo-Saxon nations such as the United Kingdom, Australia, and Canada, adopted a different approach to the old-age income problem. The conservative parties in these countries had a much more restrictive view of the proper role of the state. The United Kingdom and the United States, both early industrializers, also had a long tradition of employer plans. A common Anglo-Saxon corporate-financial culture and extensive cross-border investments also facilitated the early spread of employer pensions to large private enterprises in Australia and Canada. The Anglo-Saxon nations were also spared the worst ravages of the Second World War. So, compared to most nations on the European continent, they entered the postwar period with far more resources in the private sector that could provide retirement incomes. Employer pension plans would thus remain a significant source of support in what came to be known as "Anglo-Saxon" as opposed to Bismarckian retirement income systems. The remainder of the book focuses on the expansion of these Anglo-Saxon systems and their response to the challenges that emerged toward the end of the twentieth century.

THE ANGLO-SAXON APPROACH TO RETIREMENT INCOME SYSTEMS: 1945–1965

The immediate postwar years did see pitched political battles in Anglo-Saxon nations over the economic role of the state. Politicians on the left generally advocated a larger government role, including larger social insurance pensions. Politicians on the right generally sought a contraction, often seeking to replace social insurance with self-reliance, employer plans, and a means-tested safety net. The actual postwar settlements varied quite a bit. Britain, at one pole, nationalized coal, steel, and other basic industries and created the National Health Service. The United States, at the other, restored corporate management of the economy, restrained its unions, and limited new social welfare initiatives.

There was far less variance in the area of government old-age pensions. Anglo-Saxon nations generally continued their prewar programs with little or no increase in benefits, but they expanded coverage to include essentially all workers. In Britain, the 1946 Basic State Pension extended its 1925 social insurance plan, which paid a flat 20 percent of the average wage, to include white-collar as well as clerical and blue-collar workers. In the United States, the critical 1950 Social Security Amendments retained prewar replacement rates—30 percent for the model average worker—while expanding coverage and easing requirements for the receipt of full benefits. And in 1952 Canada converted its 1927 means-tested benefit into a universal demogrant—a flat payment made to all elderly long-term residents (Ball 1947; Commonwealth Treasury 2001; Hannah 1986; Sass 1997; Whiteside 2002).

Given the widespread acceptance of "retirement" and the low level of government benefits, a significant expansion of employer plans was critical to the success of the Anglo-Saxon approach. Coverage rates also shot up dramatically in the postwar period. Most government workers were covered by pension plans even prior to World War II, and government employment expanded significantly in the postwar period. At most only 15 percent of the private sector workforce was covered by an employer plan at the end of the 1930s, but in the postwar period, coverage came to exceed 40 percent of private-sector workers in the United States, Great Britain, Canada, and Australia (see Figure 2.2 for the growth of coverage in the United States).

This rapid rise in coverage after World War II can be traced to three factors.[8] The first was the expansion of large corporate employers. The long postwar boom was largely driven by the growth of giant mass-production mass-distribution enterprises in both manufacturing (industries such as autos, steel, and consumer goods) and services (industries such as telecommunications, banking and insurance, transportation, and public utilities). As employer pensions had become an essential component of corporate personnel systems, coverage expanded in line with the growth of big business (Chandler 1977, 1990).

Figure 2.2 U.S. Private-Sector Workers Covered by Employer Plans, 1940–2004

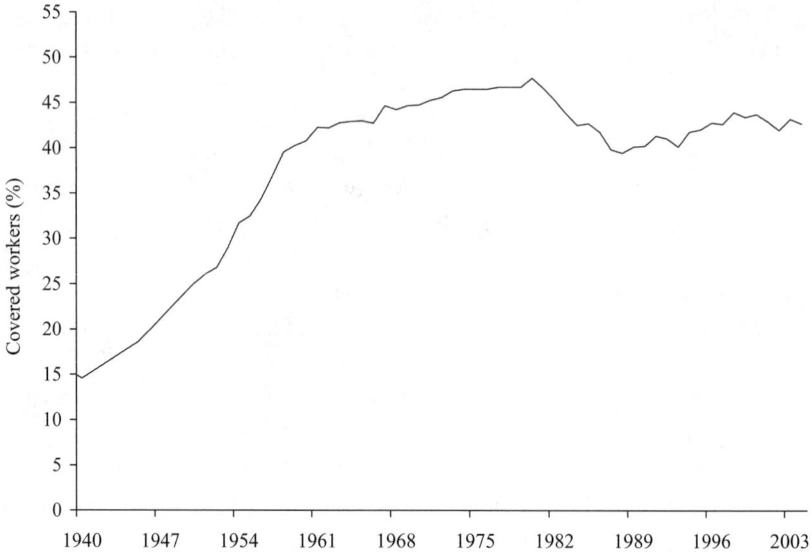

SOURCE: Authors' calculations based on Skolnik (1976); U.S. Census Bureau, Current Population Survey 1978–2005; Yohalem (1977).

   The second factor leading to increased coverage was the growing importance of pensions as tax-advantaged compensation. In all Anglo-Saxon nations, employer contributions and the investment income earned by a pension fund were tax exempt, and employees were taxed only upon the receipt of benefits. As a result, employees paid significantly less tax on compensation received in the form of deferred pension benefits than in the form of cash wages.[9] This favorable tax treatment had little effect on coverage before World War II because less than 10 percent of the adult population typically paid tax. But with the postwar growth of mass income taxation, pensions became an increasingly attractive type of compensation, particularly for high-income professionals, managers, and business owners. The foregone government revenues, or "tax expenditures," made government a major funder of employer plans and encouraged their spread.[10]
   The final factor affecting the growth in coverage was the expansion of collectively bargained plans. Labor unions and worker "friendly soci-

eties" had long sought to provide their members with old-age pensions, but the largely voluntary nature of these organizations and their limited financial resources had restricted their ability to do so. After the Second World War, however, unions throughout the industrial world found themselves in a much stronger position, and they used this new-found strength to expand old-age income benefits within the larger postwar political settlement. In continental Europe, they successfully pressed for expanded government pensions and mandatory employment-based plans that provided supplementary top-ups. In Anglo-Saxon nations, the unions negotiated generous employer plans, often with the help of the government. In the United States, the big industrial unions won generous pensions in 1949 and 1950 as part of a political settlement that included long-term labor agreements, controls on labor militancy, and the passage of the 1950 Social Security Amendments. In the United Kingdom, unions in the 1950s won generous pensions in Britain's nationalized industries from a Conservative government intent on strengthening the role of employer plans and forestalling the expansion of public programs (Hannah 1986; Sass 1997; Whiteside 2002).

THE EXPANSION OF ANGLO-SAXON RETIREMENT INCOME SYSTEMS: 1965–1980

The Anglo-Saxon approach to the retirement income problem had clearly taken root by the mid-1960s, but the results were limited. Employer plans covered half the workforce at best. Many covered workers would quit or lose their jobs before gaining a pension benefit. Others would see their plans go bust and their benefits lose much or all of their value. As public pensions provided meager, even welfare-level benefits, old-age remained a stage of life generally characterized by a sharp decline in living standards. Women, in particular, were poorly served. They generally accrued little or no employer pension benefits on their own, and benefits earned by their husbands typically came to an end when the husbands died.

In response to these shortcomings, Anglo-Saxon governments launched a series of initiatives to enlarge and strengthen their retirement income systems. This expansion largely came between 1965 and 1980

at the end of the long postwar prosperity. It included both significant increases in government benefits and initiatives designed to make employer pensions so secure and broadly distributed that they functioned as an
earnings-related second tier in the national retirement income system.

The United States expanded its public programs for the elderly between 1965 and 1972. In 1965, Congress enacted Medicare (medical
insurance for the elderly); in 1972, it sharply increased Social Security
benefits to a 42-percent earnings replacement rate for the benchmark
average earner. Canada in the late 1960s lowered the age of eligibility for the government's old-age demogrant from 70 to 65 and introduced an earnings-related social insurance pension program. For the
benchmark average earner, the combined benefit would replace about
43 percent of preretirement earnings—essentially the same as in the expanded U.S. Social Security program. Australia in the 1970s increased
its means-tested benefit for the elderly from 20 to 25 percent of average
male earnings (equal to about a third of the average wage). It also lib-
eralized access to the point where half of the elderly qualified for a full
allowance and 90 percent for at least a partial benefit. Also in the 1970s,
the United Kingdom increased its flat social insurance benefit to 25
percent of average earnings and introduced a separate earnings-related
social insurance pension. When the earnings-related program matured
in 1998, the two government pensions combined would replace a bit
less than 45 percent of the wages of the benchmark average earner.

In the United States and Canada, the government sought to strength-
en the employer component of the retirement income system by imposing an extensive set of regulations on tax-favored plans. Government
officials had taken note of the large and growing size of its pension "tax
expenditures."[11] Such a large apparent revenue loss could only be justi-
fied by a comparable contribution to public welfare. And this would
be accomplished only if employer plans allowed a large portion of the
workforce to shift income from their years of employment to their years
of retirement. In exchange for government tax benefits, the Canadian
Pension Benefits Acts of 1965–1967 (enacted at the national and provincial level) and the U.S. Employee Retirement Income Security Act
of 1974 (ERISA) established new vesting, funding, and fiduciary standards for employer plans.

Government vesting requirements insisted that covered workers be
given a "vested" right to a pension within a specified amount of time.

The regulations allowed different vesting schedules, but the most popular was full vesting after 10 years for workers age 45 or over in Canada and after 10 years in the United States. The vesting requirement meant that a much larger share of the workforce would get at least a small employer pension to supplement their government benefits. As expanding coverage beyond large employers and unionized workers appeared unlikely, vesting seemed the most effective way to expand the contribution of employer plans to retirement income security.[12]

The Canadian Pension Benefits Acts and ERISA also imposed a set of funding requirements on employer plans to increase benefit security. In the earliest plans, employers had merely paid benefits to retirees as an ongoing, operating expense. If the employer went bust, so would the benefits of current and future pensioners. In the 1920s and 1930s, however, sponsors came to recognize that pension benefits were properly treated as part of an active worker's current compensation. Employers thus recognized the accrual of pension benefits by the active workforce, not benefits paid out to retirees, as their current operating pension expense. Some employers recorded this expense in a book reserve, an accounting entry that recognized the obligation and allocated a portion of the sponsor's net worth to offset the liability. Most governments, however, denied employers favorable tax treatment for book-reserve funding. Employers in these nations generally funded their plans externally. The largest employers set up separate pension funds; smaller employers generally used insurance companies, which developed a variety of deferred annuity products for employer plans.[13]

ERISA and the Pension Benefits Acts also required employers to fully fund their plans over a period of time. When most plans were created, employers gave their existing workers pension credit for service in the past. This created substantial liabilities before the pension fund had any assets at all. The failure of the Studebaker plan in 1963 dramatically illustrated the vulnerability of this arrangement. ERISA thus required employers to fund such shortfalls within 30 years and the Canadian Pension Benefits Acts required funding within 15 years. ERISA also made employers liable for any shortfall up to 30 percent of their net worth, effectively funding the plan up to that level with the equity of the sponsor. It also created the Pension Benefit Guaranty Corporation (PBGC), which protected benefits up to a specified level in plans that went bust, primarily by imposing levies on the continuing plans.[14]

The United States and Canada also imposed new requirements on plan governance. Trust law, which had previously governed fiduciary conduct, assumed a community of interest between the grantor (the employer) and the beneficiary (the worker) and imposed fiduciary requirements only on trustees. In pension plans, the misconduct was primarily done by the corporate and union grantors, not the trustees. To protect the interests of workers, Canada required at least one trustee to be independent of the sponsor. ERISA defined a variety of "prohibited transactions" and required everyone associated with a plan, from the trustees (typically officers of the sponsor) to their consultants and agents, to act solely in the interest of the beneficiaries. These provisions effectively outlawed investments designed to advance the interests of corporate and union sponsors (Coward 1995; Hannah 1986; Sass 1997).

The United Kingdom took a different tack to strengthening employer plans. The earnings-related public pension plan, added atop the universal flat basic pension, was the government's primary lever. Unlike public programs in nearly all other nations, the earnings-related plan was designed primarily as a residual plan, for those without employer coverage. Employers with plans that provided pensions that were comparable to the government's earnings-related benefits, including to workers who left prior to qualifying for a full vested employer plan benefit, could "contract out" of the new program. Since their plans took on this pension obligation, they received a "rebate" of the social insurance tax that funded the new government benefit. The government then encouraged employers to contract out by setting the rebate of social insurance taxes above the employer's estimated cost of providing the benefit.[15]

Australia took a third approach to expanding employer plans. The Labor party had long advocated increasing public pensions and replacing the country's 1908 means-tested program with a social insurance pension plan. But oil shocks, stagflation, and the general weakening of the Australian economy had effectively blocked these options. So when Labor came to power in 1983, it pushed for the expansion of employer plans as an alternate source of old-age income. Substituting pension contributions for increased cash wages would also increase national saving and help the government achieve more immediate macroeconomic policy objectives: reductions in consumer demand, inflation, interest rates, and the nation's widening trade deficit. Together with the unions, the government succeeded in including pension benefits in the

1986 standard labor contract negotiated at the national level by labor and management representatives (Bateman and Piggot 2001a; Commonwealth Treasury 2001).

Australia's national bargaining system could not impose a nation-wide defined-benefit pension program, as seen in various continental nations. Coverage nevertheless reached 72 percent of wage and salary workers by the end of the decade. The model contract included a uniform 3 percent "award superannuation" contribution in lieu of a comparable increase in wages across all industries and firms. The plans to emerge were thus defined contribution arrangements.[16] To strengthen the new system as a broad-based source of old-age income, the government also enacted regulations that required full and immediate vesting of award superannuation contributions, equal labor-management representation on the boards overseeing the multiemployer "industry funds," and the "prudent man" fiduciary standard to govern investment management.[17]

Retirement Income Systems at the End of the Age of Expansion

The expanded retirement income systems that emerged by the end of the postwar boom—both the government-dominated "Bismarckian" systems and the mixed "Anglo-Saxon" systems—redressed a major shortcoming of the modern industrial economy. Industrialization has been an enormous economic achievement. Incomes rose dramatically as production moved out of the household into larger economic enterprises. Workers had typically enjoyed rising incomes over much of their working careers, but as they grew old, they lost their economic footing, becoming a distinctively poor and dependent population. Through the middle of the twentieth century, the elderly had largely relied for their livelihood on meager wages, contributions to the household budget from children who continued to live with them, support from children who took them into their own homes, or minimal public welfare or social insurance benefits.

The expansion of national retirement income systems during the long postwar boom allowed the elderly to maintain a reasonable approximation of their preretirement living standard for the first time in history. After adjusting for a lower tax burden, reduced expenses, smaller household size, and greater opportunities for leisure and home production, the disposable income of retirees was not significantly lower than that of working-age adults. Employer pension incomes tend to decline over time due to the erosive impact of inflation and the cessation of benefits in many cases with the death of the wage earner. This created financial difficulties in many Anglo-Saxon nations at the end of life, especially for older women. Anglo-Saxon systems also had greater disparities in the distribution of old-age income. Nevertheless, these systems provided a far more rational distribution of income across a worker's lifespan.[18]

Thus, the picture around 1980 was as follows: in the United States and other Anglo-Saxon nations, expanded government pensions had pulled the bulk of the elderly out of poverty and generally assured a modest level of comfort, though not the standard of living most had enjoyed during their working years. Employer plans functioned as a broad-based earnings-related "second tier," allowing a significant portion of the elderly to approximate their preretirement standard of living. Employer pensions were concentrated in the middle and upper end of the income distribution. Those at the bottom relied on government benefits for nearly all of their old-age income.

As shown in Figure 2.3, the source of retirement income in the United States, the United Kingdom, and Canada differed fundamentally from that in the Bismarckian systems. In the three Anglo-Saxon countries, the capital market provided 40 percent or more of the income for older people. Of this 40 percent, roughly half came from funded employer plans and half came from the return on individually held assets. The income of the elderly in Bismarckian systems—other than the Netherlands, which prefunds its quasi-public "second-tier" program—came almost entirely from pay-as-you-go government transfers (see Figure 2.3).

These expanded retirement income systems were clearly expensive. While costs varied from one nation to the next, Bismarckian programs toward the end of the twentieth century generally required annual contributions equal to at least 20 percent of covered earnings. In the United States, contributions to the Social Security old-age income program were about half that amount, pension tax expenditures about a quarter of the Social Security contribution, and contributions to employer plans about 7 to 8 percent of covered payroll.[19]

Soon after these new systems took root, it became clear that the cost of pay-as-you-go government plans would dramatically rise in the

Figure 2.3 Disposable Income by Source, Age 65+, in Eight OECD Countries, 1990s

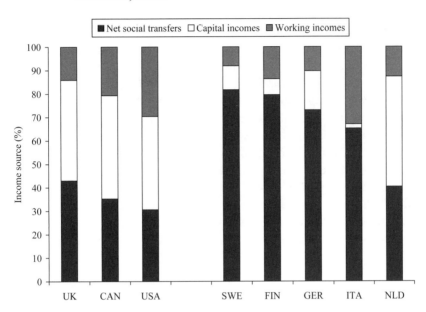

NOTE: Data for Germany and Italy are from the 1980s.
SOURCE: Yamada (2002).

future. Rapid population aging will place enormous pressure on public old-age pension programs in Anglo-Saxon and especially in Bismarckian systems. Advance-funded employer plans, as a result, appeared increasingly attractive.

Structural economic shifts, however, seriously weakened employer plans in the years after 1980. Global competition and the increased uncertainty created by the higher technical level of production undermined the market power of large corporate and union pension sponsors, which reduced their ability to underwrite and manage long-term retirement income programs. Globalization, higher education, higher technology, and the entry of married women into the paid workforce also undermined the career employment model in favor of shorter, intermediate-duration relationships. This was especially so among the higher paid workers that employer plans target. Employers would thus find far less justification for maintaining their traditional defined-benefit pension plans, which function as a reward for career employment.

Since 1980, national retirement income systems have been highly schizophrenic. The elderly have enjoyed the ample incomes provided by the expansion of public and employer programs prior to 1980. At the same time, policymakers and younger cohorts have increasingly focused on the harsh implications of rapid population aging and the withdrawal of employer interest in supporting retirement income programs. The challenge all nations now face is how best to maintain the poverty reduction and income smoothing achievements of the current system while minimizing burdens on the active population. The next chapter will review reforms to the U.S. system to date. It will then introduce the three main proposals for structurally reforming the program, all of which include investments in equities as part of the solution. The following chapters then review the experience of three Anglo-Saxon systems that have reformed their systems along the lines of these proposals.

Notes

1. These continental systems included both governmental and quasi-governmental programs. See Whiteside (2002).
2. For the growth of such organizations, see Chandler (1977, 1990).
3. Early pensions were also often provided to war veterans, but the provision of these pensions is most usefully viewed as a response to unique events rather than a solution to a persistent economic problem.
4. There were earlier plans for government employees, especially in the military. The British eighteenth-century plan for customs officials is generally seen as the precursor to later civil servant plans. The 1859 plan, however, extended pensions throughout the civil service and provided a template widely imitated by other large employers, both public and private (Raphael 1964).
5. Scaled to current U.S. earnings in 2003, the British program guaranteed the elderly an annual income between $7,240 and $11,950 (between one-fifth and one-third of average male earnings in 2003 of $36,200). Note, however, that a much larger percentage of incomes in the past were used to purchase necessities. Food, clothing, and shelter absorbed over 80 percent of a "middle income" family's expenditures in 1918, compared to less than half in 1988 (Brown 1994). Benefits in the Australian program were similar to those in the United Kingdom but granted at age 65. The Danish program paid different amounts in different locations, reflecting the significant geographic variation in the cost of living and in the welfare allowances provided by local authorities. In Britain, this variation would be

reflected in the provision of supplementary benefits for the elderly, primarily in the area of housing and local tax relief, by local government authorities (Seager 1910; Thane 2000).

6. These earnings tests reflected both the notion that public old-age pensions were insurance against an inability to work or find employment and a Depression-era impulse to reduce the supply of labor.

7. The rule-of-thumb estimate was that old-age income would need to replace between 65 and 80 percent of preretirement earnings.

8. During World War II, the government's wage controls also provided some support for pensions. The War Labor Board, which had set legal limitations on cash wages, attempted to relieve the pressure on management and labor by permitting employers to bid for workers by offering attractive fringe benefits. Pensions cost firms little in view of the wartime excess profits tax and the ability to deduct pension contributions.

9. From the point of view of an employee, these provisions are equivalent to a tax deferral on both pension contributions and the investment earnings on those contributions. Assuming the employee remains in the same tax bracket, this is equivalent to an interest-free loan on the amount of the tax (Munnell 1982).

10. In the United States, Congress leveraged its financial stake in employer plans and in 1942 enacted nondiscrimination provisions that compelled business owners and employers to distribute benefits broadly, further expanding coverage by trading tax shelters for the well-to-do for expanded retirement income benefits for the rank-and-file.

11. The size of the pension tax expenditure is difficult to measure with any precision, but most official enumerations of government tax expenditure put pensions at the top of the list.

12. In both the United States and Canada, vesting requirements have since been significantly shortened. In addition to vesting, ERISA expanded the number of employer plan beneficiaries—specifically to elderly widows who were poorly served by earnings-based retirement income systems—by making a joint-and-survivor annuity the default annuity form. Unless specifically waived, the surviving spouse (nearly always a widow) would receive half the worker's pension, which would be actuarially reduced to pay for this survivor benefit (Coward 1995; Sass 1997).

13. Although these claims were recognized and increasingly funded by large corporate sponsors, active workers typically had a legally enforceable claim only to benefits provided by an insurance company. In uninsured plans, corporate lawyers typically defined pension benefits as a "gratuity" that the employer was under no legal obligation to provide. Prior to 1938, pension assets in the United States could be held in a revocable trust, allowing the sponsor to reclaim the assets at will. After the Second World War, the courts and then the legislatures made pension benefits a legally enforceable claim (Coward 1995; Sass 1997).

14. Under the U.S. 1942 Revenue Act, sponsors had to contribute an amount equal to benefits accrued in the current year plus an amount needed to prevent any current shortfall from widening. ERISA required such shortfalls to be amortized

over time. It also required shortfalls arising from sources such as an unexpected rise in longevity or a decline in asset returns to be funded within 15 years. In the United Kingdom, funding was largely left to the discretion of the sponsor's consulting actuary, a policy that proved generally effective in assuring the solvency of employer plans (Coward 1995; Sass 1997).

15. The United Kingdom introduced a public earnings-related pension program, with this contracting-out feature, in 1961. This Graduated Retirement Benefit plan was slight, ill-designed, and widely suspected of being a Tory political ploy rather than a bona-fide retirement income initiative. The State Earnings Related Pension Scheme (SERPS), introduced in 1978, was a far more ambitious program. In both programs, employers did not have to take on the entire pension liability. The government retained the riskier portions of the obligation, such as inflation proofing. In the SERPS program, the government set the contribution rebate at about 0.5 percentage point above the estimated private cost of providing the benefit to encourage contracting out. The cost estimate included administrative expenses, which increased costs above those of the government program, but assumed a significant use of equities in funding the benefit, which reduced costs far below the present value of the benefit discounted at the riskless government rate (Daykin 2001; Hannah 1986).

16. Essentially all U.S. collectively bargained plans had a defined-benefit rather than a defined-contribution format. This was the case even though the cost of these benefits was carefully priced at the bargaining table as equivalent to a certain amount per hour. In these U.S. negotiated plans, costs and benefits varied dramatically and the employers bore the risk that their contributions and pension fund income would be insufficient to fund the promised benefits. A nationwide agreement to contribute a fixed percentage of earnings to pension plans that covered a wide variety of employer or industry groups, even in the United States, would likely result in plans with a defined-contribution format (Sass 1997).

17. The prudent man standard is common in Anglo-Saxon trust law. In the formulation specified in ERISA, "a fiduciary shall discharge his duties with respect to a plan solely in the interest of the participants and beneficiaries and . . . with the care, skill, prudence, and diligence under the circumstances then prevailing that a prudent man acting in a like capacity and familiar with such matters would use in the conduct of an enterprise of like character and with like aims . . . " (Bateman and Piggot 2001a; Commonwealth Treasury 2001).

18. The United Kingdom is somewhat of an outlier, with the disposable income of the elderly clearly lower than that of working-age adults. But, even in the United Kingdom, the disposable income levels reported by Yamada (2000) are reasonably close.

19. In the United States, the contribution rate for Social Security old-age, survivors, and disability insurance is currently 12.4 percent of covered earnings, split evenly between employers and employees, realizing $511 billion in 2005; the pension tax expenditure for 2005, as reported by the Office of Management and Budget (2005) (for employer plans, Keogh plans for small businesses, and individual retirement accounts, which are primarily rollovers from employer plans) was $141 billion.

3
The Retirement Income Challenge Facing the United States

The U.S. retirement income system, like the systems in other industrial nations, faces major demographic and economic challenges going forward. As discussed in the introduction, population aging over the next quarter century will raise the cost of promised Social Security benefits far above projected revenues. Eliminating the shortfall requires some combination of higher taxes, lower benefits, and/or the introduction of equity investments with their higher returns, albeit with greater risk. Complicating the challenge of restoring balance to Social Security is a major shift in the nature of employer-sponsored retirement income plans. In 1980, most covered workers were in traditional defined-benefit pension plans, which provide lifelong benefits typically based on final salary and years of service. In such plans, the employer managed the program and bore key risks, such as the risk that investment returns prove inadequate or that retirees live longer than expected. Today, employers typically offer defined-contribution plans—primarily 401(k) plans—where the employee makes the decisions and bears all the risk. While 401(k) plans are better for mobile employees in that they can take their accumulations with them as they move from job to job, the ultimate level of retirement income has become much more uncertain. Reform proposals for Social Security must therefore be considered in the context of the increased risk that workers now face in their 401(k) plans.

This chapter describes the evolution of the U.S. public and employer-sponsored retirement system since 1980 and the primary options put forward as potential solutions to Social Security's funding deficit.

THE U.S. RETIREMENT SYSTEM

The United States has a retirement income system with relatively modest public pensions and significant employer plans. Like other Anglo-Saxon nations, the United States expanded both public and employer programs at the end of the long prosperity that followed the end of the Second World War. After Congress enacted Medicare in 1965 and increased Social Security benefits in 1972, the bulk of the elderly were lifted out of poverty and assured a modestly comfortable standard of living. After the enactment of ERISA in 1974, employer pensions became a reasonably secure and widespread source of old-age income, primarily for middle- and upper-income workers. Income from government and employer plans, along with rising home ownership, has allowed much of the elderly to maintain a reasonable approximation of preretirement living standards.

The Role of Social Security in the U.S. Retirement Income System

Social Security has been the largest source of old-age income in the United States over the past quarter century. Social Security benefits are critically important for low-wage workers because they have virtually no other source of retirement income. Today, as in 1980, Social Security accounts for more than 80 percent of income in the lowest quintile of elderly households compared with only 19 percent in the highest. Even in the middle-income quintile, Social Security provides two-thirds of income (Figure 3.1).[1]

The Social Security benefit formula has remained essentially unchanged since the expansion of the program in the 1970s. (See Box 3.1 for a description of how Social Security benefits are calculated.) The standard measure of the generosity of such programs is the replacement rate of a hypothetical average earner. The replacement rate is the benefit as a percent of preretirement earnings. The hypothetical average earner is a worker who consistently earns the national average wage and retires at age 65.[2] The Social Security Administration calculates replacement rates for hypothetical low, medium (average), and high earners—workers who effectively earn 45 percent, 100 percent, and 160 percent of national average earnings over their working careers and retire at age 65.

Figure 3.1 Sources of Retirement Income in the United States, by Income Quintile, 2004

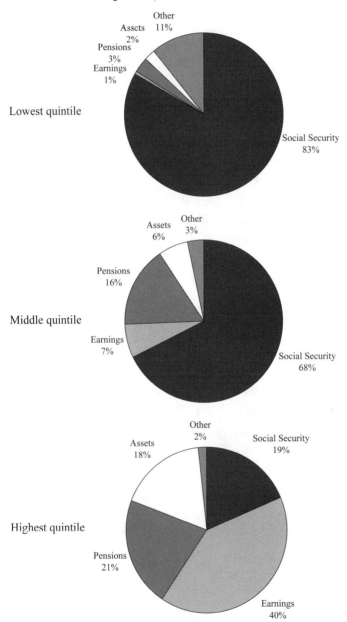

SOURCE: Authors' calculations based on U.S. Census Bureau, Current Population Survey (2005).

Box 3.1 The Calculation of Social Security Benefits

The primary insurance amount (PIA) is the benefit a worker would receive at the normal retirement age. The calculation of a worker's PIA involves three steps:

1) Earnings prior to age 60 are restated in terms of current wages. This is done by indexing those earnings by wage growth up to age 60. Wages after age 60 are not indexed.

2) The highest 35 years of adjusted and unadjusted earnings are then averaged and divided by 12 to give average indexed monthly earnings (AIME).

3) Finally, the PIA is produced by applying three different replacement rates to different portions of the worker's AIME. The "bend points" dividing AIME into these three tranches are set percentages of national average earnings (NAE) in the year the worker reaches age 60. Specifically, a worker's PIA replaces

   - 90 percent of AIME up to 22 percent of NAE in the year s/he turns 60,
   - 32 percent of AIME between 22 and 133 percent of NAE that year, and
   - 15 percent of any AIME in excess of 133 percent of NAE that year.

For workers reaching age 60 in 2004, the PIA is the sum of

   - 90 percent of the worker's first $656 of AIME, plus
   - 32 percent of AIME between $656 and $3,955, plus
   - 15 percent of any AIME in excess of $3,955.

The worker's PIA is continually recalculated as long as the individual remains employed. It is also indexed to prices from age 62.

Table 3.1 U.S. Social Security Replacement Rates for Hypothetical Workers, 2006

Earner	Career average earnings	Replacement rate (%)	
		Age 62	Age 65
Low	45% of national avg. earnings	42	56
Medium	100% of national avg. earnings	31	41
High	160% of national avg. earnings	26	35
Maximum		22	29

SOURCE: U.S. Social Security Administration (2006).

It also calculates replacement rates for a hypothetical maximum earner, whose wages consistently equal the maximum amount covered by the program. These replacement rates for 2006 are given in Table 3.1.

Retired workers do not need 100 percent of their preretirement earnings to maintain their preretirement standard of living. They no longer pay Social Security payroll tax, often pay less in income tax, have typically paid off their mortgage, no longer need to save for retirement, nor need to support their children. Estimates of the amount of income needed to maintain preretirement living standards typically range from 65 to 85 percent of preretirement earnings. The hypothetical replacement rates in Table 3.1 indicate that Social Security satisfies a large portion of the retirement income needs of low-wage workers. Medium and high earners must clearly supplement their Social Security income, primarily through employer plan benefits, to maintain their preretirement standard of living.

The replacement rates in Table 3.1 are hypothetical. They depend on several clearly unrealistic assumptions. Workers do not earn a constant percentage of the national average wage over the course of their careers. Recently retired men, in fact, have averaged 6 years of zero earnings from age 22 to the year they claim benefits. Women have averaged 13 years of zero earnings (U.S. Social Security Administration 2004). Most workers also claim benefits well before age 65. In 2003, 59 percent of women and 53 percent of men claimed benefits at age 62. And while the hypothetical rates are typically given for individuals, most people enter retirement as couples.

Estimates of actual Social Security replacement rates are nevertheless quite close to what the policy model suggests, as shown in Table 3.2.[3] Retirement earlier than the Normal Retirement Age lowers actual

Table 3.2 Actual Median Social Security Replacement Rates in the United States

Household type	Benefits as a percent of indexed lifetime earnings
Couples	44.1
Spouse has no earnings	58.0
Spouse has earnings	41.1
Single	45.2
Men	38.7
Women	48.7
All	44.4

SOURCE: Munnell and Soto (2005a).

replacement rates. On the other hand, the years out of the labor force reduces lifetime earnings and this reduction, given the program's progressive benefit formula, raises replacement rates. In addition, Social Security gives spouses the greater of their own earned benefit or half of their spouse's benefit, which raises the replacement rate of couples.

For single individuals, the median Social Security replacement rate is 45 percent—quite close to the hypothetical rate. Men have lower replacement rates because they have above-average earnings and the program's progressive benefit formula replaces a smaller percentage of above-average earnings; single women, conversely, have below-average earnings and higher replacement rates. For couples, the median Social Security replacement rate is 44 percent. Not surprisingly, earnings replacement is sharply higher for couples where only one spouse works. As married women have gone to work, they often increase the household's preretirement earnings without raising its Social Security benefits, since the woman's own earned benefit is often less than half her husband's benefit. The result has been a 41 percent replacement rate for couples where both spouses have earnings.

Social Security replacement rates for most household types thus appear quite close to the hypothetical 42 percent rate. This level of earnings replacement is generally seen as providing a solid base upon which most retirees can add income from other sources for a relatively secure retirement.

But this level of earnings replacement is scheduled to sharply decline, as noted in Chapter 1. After the rise in the normal retirement age, the deduction of increased Medicare premiums, and the taxation of benefits under the personal income tax, the replacement rate for the hypothetical medium earner will be substantially lower in, say, 2030 than it is today.

The Role of Employer Plans in the U.S. Retirement Income System

Employer retirement plans, especially after the enactment of ERISA in 1974, function as the nation's primary supplement to Social Security for middle- and high-income workers. Most government workers and about half of the private sector workforce—essentially the better paid half—participate in an employer-sponsored plan. In 1980, most such workers were covered by a defined-benefit pension plan that paid benefits at retirement in the form of a lifetime annuity. The payment is typically calculated as a percentage of final salary for each year of service, say 1.5 percent, so workers with 20 years would receive 30 percent of final salary for as long as they live.[4] The employer finances these benefits by making pretax contributions into a pension fund; employees typically do not contribute.

For the steady employee who remains with one firm, defined-benefit plans provide a stream of monthly benefits that replaces a significant portion of earnings at retirement. The major drawback is that mobile employees forfeit some or all future pension income when they move from job to job. Despite this limitation, employer pensions account for about a fifth of the income of the elderly, and about a quarter of that income other than earnings from work. Among households with employer pension income, Social Security and employer plan benefits at retirement replace 70 percent of preretirement earnings for the median single individual and 63 percent for the median couple (Table 3.3). This level of earnings replacement is sufficient to maintain a rough approximation of preretirement living standards.

Employers supported these plans because they helped manage their workforce. As discussed in Chapter 2, defined-benefit pension plans encourage long tenure and efficient retirement.[5] To fund these plans, employers typically contributed between 7 and 8 percent of payroll. The plan trustees (typically officers of the employer) then held the assets and directed the investments, with the employer retaining the risk that the assets in the plan would not be sufficient to pay out promised

Table 3.3 Actual Replacement Rates in the United States for Median Couples and Singles, with and without Pension Income

Household type	Replacement rate (%) Social Security + pension
Couples	
Without pension	43.0
With pension	63.3
Single	
Without pension	46.2
With pension	70.4

NOTE: The replacement rates in this table define retirement income as Social Security benefits, employer pensions, the annuitized value of employer defined-contribution balances, and for those with pension coverage, the annuitized value of Individual Retirement Account (IRA) balances. IRA balances are included for those with pension coverage, as most IRA balances have been created as a result of rollovers from employer plans. The replacement rates in this table define preretirement income as AIME plus earnings above the cap and returns on financial assets.
SOURCE: Munnell and Soto (2005b).

benefits. ERISA required the employer to pay down shortfalls within 15 or 30 years, depending on the source. Should a plan terminate with insufficient assets, the PBGC, created by ERISA, insured benefits up to specified limits.[6]

THE REFORM OF THE U.S. RETIREMENT INCOME SYSTEM SINCE 1980

Soon after the expansion of the nation's retirement income system, it became clear that powerful demographic and economic forces were undermining the system's long-term finances. Serious solvency problems emerged in both Social Security and employer plans. Employers also found traditional defined-benefit pension plans unsuited to the more fluid and volatile global high-tech economy and instead opted for new and largely untested defined-contribution retirement plans.

Shoring Up the Solvency of Employer Defined-Benefit Plans

ERISA's regulation of pension funding followed the "best practice" of the pension actuaries. In particular, it regulated solvency by asking whether a plan's assets were sufficient to pay promised future benefits, given the expected return on those assets. But in the recessions of 1980–1982, large funding deficits suddenly emerged, exposing serious inadequacies in this approach. The primary reason why these large deficits appeared so suddenly was because employer plans invest a substantial portion of their assets in equities. The expected return on equities is far greater than that on bonds, which makes a plan far more affordable, but equities are risky (see Box 3.2). Even if equities deliver their expected return in the long run, the value of a plan's assets can suddenly fall. Often the fall in asset prices triggers a cut in *expected* returns, which sharply raises the present value of the plan's distant pension obligations. In the actuarial funding approach, which ERISA had adopted, the sponsor functioned as the plan's financial guarantor. When "risk happened," employers were required to increase their contributions and gradually bring the plan back into balance. But, rather than being able to backstop their plans, many large sponsors themselves went bankrupt in the recessions of the early 1980s.

The plan of a bankrupt sponsor is terminated, and any unfunded liabilities are transferred to the PBGC. Without the employer as the financial guarantor, only low-risk bonds can be used to satisfy the liabilities of a terminated plan. The pensions are much lower than in an ongoing plan, as benefits are based on earnings at the time of the termination, not at retirement or some later date. But, as bonds carry an interest rate well below the expected return on equities, each dollar of future pension benefits requires more assets to make the plan solvent. To protect workers (and the PBGC) in the event of a termination, Congress reformed the rules of employer plan funding in 1987. It required sponsors to calculate the plan's termination liability—the present value of currently accrued benefits discounted to the present using the interest rate on low-risk bonds as the discount rate. If the plan's assets were less than 90 percent of its termination liability, the sponsor had to eliminate the deficit within five years.[7]

Box 3.2 Asset Returns and Risks

Stocks have historically delivered much higher returns than bonds. Over the period from 1926 to 2002, stocks returned 7.2 percent, after adjusting for inflation, compared with 2.4 percent for intermediate government bonds (see table below).

But returns are not the whole story. Stocks are much riskier, as seen in the standard deviations of returns reported in the table. Stocks can be expected to outperform bonds over the long term, but the performance of the stock market is very uncertain. For any given 10-year period over the past 75 years, investors have had a 25 percent chance of realizing lower returns from a portfolio of Standard and Poor's stocks than from a portfolio of government bonds (MaCurdy and Shoven 2001).

The higher expected return on stocks, in fact, is due to their greater risk. Investors are risk-averse and demand an "equity premium" to hold stocks instead of bonds. If stocks were not priced in a way that produced a higher expected return, investors would always choose bonds. (Some economists [e.g., Mehra and Prescott 1985] have concluded that the rate of return on stocks is greater than can be explained by their greater riskiness).

Annual Returns on Financial Instruments in the United States, 1926–2002

Financial instrument	Real rate of return (%)	Standard deviation
Equities[a]	7.2	20.5
Long-term corporate bonds	2.9	8.7
Intermediate government bonds	2.4	5.8
U.S. Treasury bills	1.8	3.2
Memo:		
Inflation	3.0	4.4

[a] Stocks refer to the returns on large company stocks. Over the same period, the return and standard deviation on small company stocks was somewhat higher: a 12.5 percent return with a standard deviation of 33.2 percent.
SOURCE: Ibbotson Associates (2003). Based on copyrighted work by Ibbotson and Sinquefield. All rights reserved. Used with permission.

The Shift to Defined-Contribution Employer Plans

Maintaining the solvency of defined-benefit plans has been the most difficult employer plan challenge since 1980. But the most important change was the shift from defined-benefit to defined-contribution plans (most often a 401[k]). By any criterion—assets, benefits, participation, or contributions—defined-contribution plans grew enormously between 1979 and 2000 (Figure 3.2). In contrast to defined-benefit plans, defined-contribution plans are like savings accounts. Generally the employee, and often the employer, contributes a specified percentage of earnings into the worker's individual account. These contributions are invested, usually at the direction of the employee, mostly in mutual funds consisting of stocks and bonds. Upon retirement, the worker generally receives the balance in the account as a lump sum.

The defining characteristic of 401(k) plans is that the burden of providing for retirement is largely shifted to the worker. The employee

Figure 3.2 Defined-Contribution Plans as a Share of Total Pension Plans in the United States, 1979 and 2000

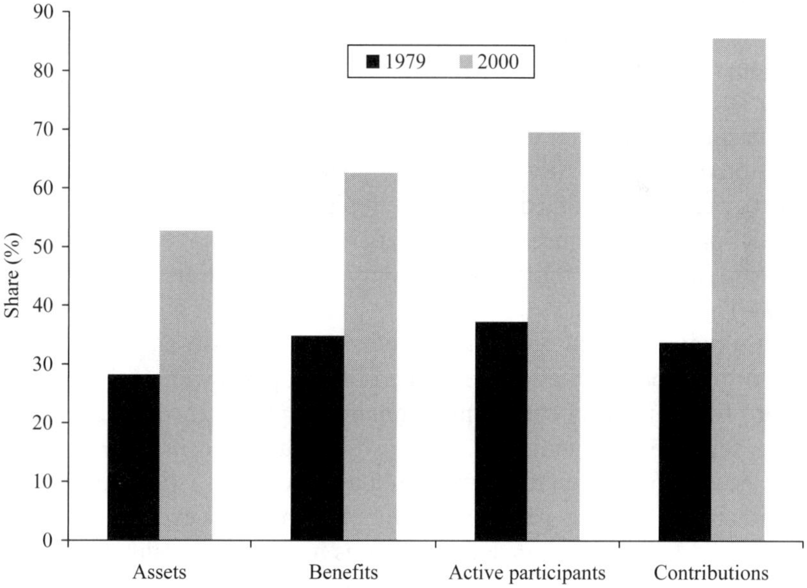

SOURCE: U.S. Department of Labor (2004, 2005).

decides whether or not to participate, how much to contribute, how to invest the assets, and how to use the assets at retirement. In addition, workers can often access their 401(k) assets before retirement, adding another element of individual responsibility.

The shift to 401(k)s was led by a surge in new plan formation in the 1980s, a virtual halt in the formation of new defined-benefit plans, and a spike in terminations during the late 1980s.[8] Defined-benefit plans were rarely converted to a 401(k), particularly among large plans. The most likely explanation for this reluctance is the enormous turmoil caused when mid- and late-career employees lose benefits in such a conversion.

Why did 401(k) plans spread so rapidly after 1980 while defined-benefit plans languished? A key factor in the enormous appeal of 401(k) plans to employees was the ability to gain control of their retirement planning. They could make tax-deductible contributions, have discretion over the amount saved and the investment allocation, and see their accounts grow. Most plans allowed loans and withdrawals, and young mobile workers—the primary participants in the early expansion of the 401(k)—could take their 401(k) accumulations with them as they moved from job to job.

From the employers' perspective, 401(k) plans offered a form of pension that their workers clearly appreciated. Moreover, the employer no longer bears the risks involved in funding future retirement annuities. The cost of a 401(k) plan was highly predictable, which became increasingly important during the 1980s as the economic environment became more competitive. The out-of-pocket cost of a 401(k) plan was also lower than that of a defined-benefit plan—in the order of 2 to 3 percent of payroll. Advances in computer and communications technology also greatly simplified the cost of administering the individual accounts in a 401(k) plan.

Employment and high-value production was also shifting to sectors of the labor market where defined-benefit plans were less useful as a tool for structuring employment relationships. Defined-benefit plans are a sensible arrangement for large well-established firms with long-service employees, but they are ill-suited to industries where companies come and go and the workforce is mobile. Indeed they penalize what employers and workers in such industries increasingly valued—mobility and flexibility. Several studies find that changes in industry composition, unionization, and firm size account for about half the decline in defined-benefit coverage (see, e.g., Andrews 1985; Gustman and Stein-meier 1992; and Ippolito 1995).

The increasingly complicated government regulation of defined-benefit plans also caused new companies, and many existing small firms, to opt for 401(k)s. In addition to ERISA, a large and complicated set of requirements in its own right, Congress in the 1980s repeatedly imposed new burdens, such as the new funding obligations and sharply increased PBGC premiums. These regulations made pensions, which are supported by federal income tax preferences, fairer and more secure, but they also made defined-benefit plans more complex and costly. The cumulative impact of the legislative changes has greatly increased the relative costs of defined-benefit plans, especially for small companies.[9]

A major consequence in the shift from defined-benefit pensions to 401(k)s was that employers became far less involved in the retirement income system. They generally provide a matching contribution for workers who participate, typically 50 percent on contributions up to 6 percent of earnings (Profit Sharing/401[k] Council of America 2005). But they typically outsource plan administration and investment management to financial services firms, bear none of the risks, and conduct no actuarial reviews of the retirement planning effort. Employers get some personnel benefits from offering a 401(k), attracting a more thrifty and presumably more diligent workforce (Ippolito 1998), but employers are no longer the driving force behind these plans. The initiative in retirement planning has clearly shifted to their employees and to the government, with its interest in increasing retirement saving through the offer of tax benefits.

Restoring Solvency to the Social Security Program

The expansion of Social Security benefits in 1972 came just eight years after the baby boom came to an end in 1964. Fertility rates fell from 3.6 children per woman in 1960 to 1.8 in 1975. It took time for policymakers to conclude that the fertility decline was permanent and would create a major financing problem for Social Security. By the early 1980s, however, the threat was clearly understood. The Social Security actuary estimated the program's deficit at 1.8 percent of taxable payroll over the 75-year planning horizon.

In response, the National Commission on Social Security Reform was formed, headed by Alan Greenspan. The commission represented a broad cross section of political opinion, and its 1983 report presented a series of reforms, endorsed by either the whole commission or a majority of its members that would restore solvency over the 75-year horizon. The key solvency reforms that Congress enacted into law included (National Commission on Social Security Reform 1983):

Increased funding

- Accelerated the introduction of scheduled future tax increases. Social Security retirement benefits in 1982 were funded by a 9.15 percent tax on wages, split evenly between workers and employers. The tax was quickly raised to the current 10.6 percent.

- Increased the payroll tax paid by the self-employed to equal the total employer-employee tax on wage-and-salary workers.

- Extended coverage to nonprofit and new Federal government workers.

Decreased benefits

- Cut future benefits by increasing the Normal Retirement Age. Congress increased the normal retirement age from 65 (for those reaching age 62 prior to the year 2000) to age 67 (for those who reach 62 in 2022 or after).

- Subjected half the benefits of higher-income beneficiaries to income taxation, with the proceeds returned to the Social Security program.

The design of the system has changed little since these reforms. Since 1983, the most important changes have perhaps been the decision to subject 85 percent of the benefits of higher income beneficiaries to income taxation, up from 50 percent, and the elimination of the earnings test, in 2000, for workers older than the normal retirement age.

THE CHALLENGE GOING FORWARD

The reforms enacted since 1980 strengthened the solvency of both Social Security and employer defined-benefit plans for a time. But, by the early years of the twenty-first century, both faced solvency problems quite similar to those addressed in the 1980s. Defined-contribution plans, now the dominant form of employer retirement programs, are solvent by definition, but their ability to deliver adequate old-age incomes, especially given the scheduled decline in Social Security replacement rates, has emerged as a serious new problem. On the positive side, the system has changed in ways that encourage workers to extend their careers and shorten their retirements, which could have an important beneficial effect on the retirement income problem.

The Uncertain Future of Employer Plans

The reforms enacted to shore up employer defined-benefit plans did little to increase the flow of resources into the system from the mid-1980s through the end of the century. The funding ratios that the government used to measure solvency were strong. The stock market boomed, which drove up the value of pension fund assets. The returns on both stocks and bonds were high, which kept the present value of future obligations low. But Congress also strictly limited a sponsor's ability to contribute to a "fully funded" pension plan. As a result, relatively little new money flowed into the system.

After the turn of the century, the economy slid into recession and the old solvency problems returned. Total underfunding in employer defined-benefit plans reached an estimated $400 billion, and the average funding ratio fell to 76 percent by year-end 2002. Under the new funding rules, this low level of funding triggered a sharp increase in required pension contributions. This demand for increased contributions in recessions, precisely when employers are financially stressed, makes the future of traditional defined-benefit plans even more uncertain (Bovbjerg 2003; WatsonWyatt 2005a).

The 401(k) plan has clearly emerged as the dominant employer plan design. Its performance as a vehicle for achieving retirement income security, however, has been disappointing. Simulations show that a worker in the middle of the earnings distribution in theory should end up with about $300,000 in his 401(k) account and/or IRA at retirement. (Most of the money in IRAs is rolled-over balances from 401(k) plans.) This amount would provide an adequate retirement income in addition to Social Security. The Federal Reserve's 2001 Survey of Consumer Finances, however, reports that the typical individual approaching retirement had only $60,000 in such accounts (Figure 3.3). Of course, many in this group may not have spent a lifetime covered by 401(k) plans. But even younger cohorts, who have grown up with 401(k) plans, do not seem to be on track for an adequate retirement income. For example, the average 401(k)/IRA holdings for those 45 to 54 are only $49,000 compared to a predicted $155,000.

A critical factor explaining these low balances is that the entire burden has shifted from the employer to the employee. In these plans, workers must decide whether or not to join, how much to contribute, how to invest the assets, when to rebalance, what to do about company stock, whether to roll over accumulations when changing jobs, and how to withdraw the money at retirement. The evidence indicates that a significant fraction of participants makes serious mistakes at every step along the way. Most importantly, a quarter of those eligible to partici-

Figure 3.3   401(k)/IRA Actual and Simulated Accumulations in the United States, by Age Group, 2001

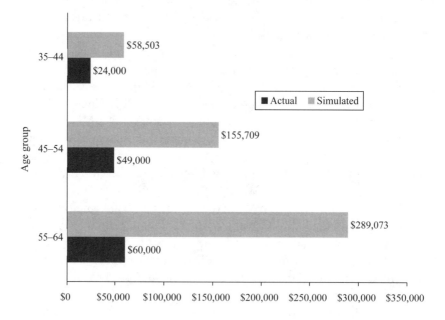

SOURCE: Munnell and Sundén (2004).

pate choose not to do so, and many cash out when they change jobs. In addition, over half fail to diversify their investments, many overinvest in company stock, and almost no participants rebalance their portfolios as they age or in response to market returns.

The basic problem is that financial decisions are difficult. Most participants lack sufficient financial experience, training, or time to figure out what to do. These plans could be greatly improved by making them easier and more automatic. Indeed, one-third of large 401(k) plans now have automatic enrollment provisions whereby employees are automatically put into the plan and must explicitly opt out if they do not want to participate (Profit Sharing/401[k] Council of America 2005). Although this and other changes may improve balances in the future, to date they remain low.

An important consequence of the shift to 401(k)s that strengthens the retirement income system has been the elimination of early retirement incentives found in defined-benefit pension plans. As discussed above, employers built incentives into their pension plans to terminate employment relationships at some targeted age. Over the last quarter of the twentieth century, sponsors commonly offered sweetened early retirement pensions to induce retirements well before age 65, the normal retirement age generally specified in such plans. These incentives helped push the average retirement age for men from age 66 in 1970 to age 63 in 1985 (see Figure 3.4).

By contrast, 401(k) plans are age-neutral. The balance in a worker's account does not change as a result of the worker reaching a particular age. Working longer will reduce the length of retirement, so a given balance would yield a higher monthly payout. It should also push up the worker's balance due to added contributions and investment earnings. These plans have no age-triggered adjustments and especially no sweeteners to induce a worker to retire early. A number of studies have shown that workers covered by a 401(k) retire about one year later than otherwise similar workers covered by traditional defined-benefit plans (Friedberg and Webb 2005; Munnell, Triest, and Jivan 2004).

The emergence of the 401(k) coincided with the stabilization of the average retirement age for U.S. men in the mid-1980s, and its slight rise since then (Figure 3.4). The shift to 401(k)s should not be seen as responsible because it takes decades for such a change to affect work-retirement decisions. The fact that the retirement income system has

Figure 3.4 Average Retirement Age of Men in the United States, 1910–2004

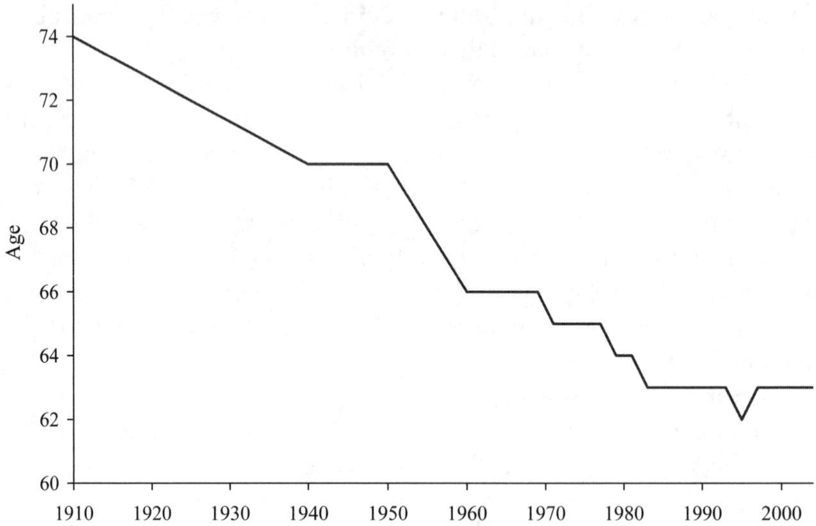

SOURCE: Burtless and Quinn (2002); authors' calculations using Bureau of Labor Statistics (2005).

become significantly more "age-neutral," however, should become increasingly important going forward.[10] To the extent that it raises the average retirement age, the shift to 401(k)s would increase the resources and reduce the burdens on the retirement income system.

The nation's employer retirement income plans have changed dramatically since 1980. The experience thus far illustrates serious difficulties in maintaining the solvency of employer defined-benefit plans and in relying on 401(k)s as a retirement income security vehicle. The elimination of early retirement incentives, however, should be an important improvement. These changes in employer plans provide a critical backdrop when considering alternative approaches to restoring solvency to Social Security.

Social Security's Long-Term Funding Shortfall

The 1983 reforms cut benefits, raised contributions, and built up the Social Security Trust Fund. The 1983 Trustees Report in fact projected a 75-year surplus equal to 0.02 percent of taxable payrolls. Nevertheless, deficits appeared almost immediately after the 1983 legislation and increased sharply in the early 1990s. The 2006 Trustees Report projects a deficit of 2.02 percent over the 75-year horizon, essentially the same as the deficit prior to the 1983 amendments (see Figure 3.5). Without any changes, Social Security can pay full benefits until 2040. Thereafter payroll taxes are sufficient to cover only about 70 percent of commitments.

Why did the balance deteriorate? Table 3.4 shows the source of the swing in the Trustee's accounts. Leading the list is the impact of changing the valuation period. That is, the 1983 Report looked at the system's finances over the period 1983–2058; the projection period for the 2006 report is 2006–2080. Each time the valuation period moves out one year, it picks up a year with a large negative balance. This is the reason why policymakers now insist on looking beyond the 75-year projection period when considering ways to restore solvency.

Figure 3.5 U.S. Social Security's 75-Year Deficit as a Percent of Taxable Payrolls, 1983–2005

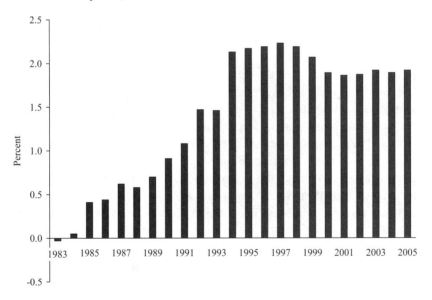

SOURCE: U.S. Social Security Administration (2006).

Table 3.4 Reasons for Change in the Actuarial Deficit of Social Security in the United States, 1983–2006

Item	Change as a percent of payroll
Actuarial balance in 1983	+0.02
Changes in actuarial balance due to	
Valuation period	−1.35
Actuarial projection methods	−0.56
Disability assumptions	−0.71
Economic assumptions	−0.33
Legislation	+0.16
Demographic assumptions	+0.76
Total change in actuarial balance[a]	−2.04
Actuarial balance in 2006	−2.02

[a] Total change in actuarial balance includes 0.02 percent that could not be attributed to listed categories.
SOURCE: Author's calculations based on 1983–2006 U.S. Social Security Trustees' Reports.

A Social Security Advisory Council, established by President Clinton in 1994, thus had to revisit the problem. As was typical, the council represented a broad cross section of political opinion. The members reached a consensus on various principles and reforms—they opposed means-testing, they thought that each generation's benefits should bear a reasonable relationship to its contributions, they favored an increase in the income taxation of benefits, and they also suggested bringing new state and local government workers into the program. A small majority would also accelerate the rise in the Normal Retirement Age and then index it to longevity. These initiatives, however, were insufficient to eliminate the program's long-term funding shortfall (U.S. 1994–1996 Advisory Council on Social Security 1997).

The council members found themselves beyond the standard approach to restoring solvency (i.e., via tax increases and benefit cuts alone). The payroll tax was already the largest federal tax by far on low- and middle-income households, and benefits would be quite low after the 1983 amendments were fully phased in. Further cuts would clearly put the standard of living of many older Americans at risk.

Rather than relying solely on higher taxes or lower benefits, members of the advisory council embraced—in one form or another—investment in equities, with their high expected returns, to help restore solvency to the nation's Social Security program. They also saw equity investment as the only way to make the Social Security benefits that younger workers would receive in retirement bear a reasonable relationship to their contributions. But the council failed to coalesce around a single consensus approach. Instead it divided into three separate camps, each advancing a distinctly different proposal with a different approach to equity investment. These three approaches define the primary options for reforming the basic design of the U.S. Social Security program.

- *Trust Fund Investment.* The "Maintenance of Benefits" plan recommended modest changes to taxes and benefits and closed the remaining gap by investing a portion of trust fund assets in equities, which promised higher expected returns, and also by increasing contributions in the out years.

- *Add-On Accounts.* The "Individual Accounts" plan proposed to achieve solvency by cutting Social Security's guaranteed benefits to fit within the existing payroll tax. In response to the sense that benefits would then be inadequate, the plan mandated an additional contribution, equal to 1.6 percent of covered earnings, to new individual retirement savings accounts. The use of individual accounts opened the door for equity investments earmarked for old-age pensions but without involving the government in the financial markets and corporate governance.

- *Carve-Out Accounts.* The "Personal Security Accounts" plan proposed to achieve solvency by cutting Social Security's guaranteed benefits and carving contributions to "Personal Security Accounts"—equal to 5 percent of covered earnings—out of the existing payroll tax. Guaranteed benefits had to be cut not just to fit within the resources provided by the current payroll tax, as in the Add-on Account approach, but even more to accommodate the 5 percent carve out. To maintain benefit adequacy, the plan relied on larger investment in equities, with their high expected returns. The reform advanced by President Bush is a descendent of this proposal.

Political considerations have largely determined the support given each proposal for incorporating equities into the Social Security program. Liberals are comfortable with government programs and prefer trust fund investment, as it maintains Social Security's currently scheduled level of guaranteed benefits. Conservatives prefer carve-out accounts, as it promises to minimize the scope of government and maximize individual self-reliance. Moderates seeking a middle ground will often opt for the add-on accounts approach, with the somewhat smaller guaranteed benefits, the addition of a limited amount of individual choice, and a politically palatable way (mandatory saving vs. higher taxes) to get more resources into the system.

Practical considerations should also influence the desirability of the three alternative approaches to reforming Social Security. Most important is how the approach to equities shapes the retirement income system. Other considerations include the cost of administering these programs, the ability to oversee their operation and restrain the power of government, and the capacity for handling the risk in equity investment. Risk management is perhaps the most critical of these pragmatic considerations. As the experience of employer defined-benefit pension plans clearly shows, the risk that comes with equity investment can radically upset a retirement income program.

CONCLUSION

The U.S. retirement income system enters the new century in an unsettled state. Social Security, the primary source of income for the majority of older Americans, lacks the resources as of 2040 to pay the full value of even the reduced benefits currently promised. This solvency problem has dominated retirement income policy debates for well over a decade, but rather than move the discussion toward consensus, the debates have generated increasingly fierce disagreements over the government's proper size and role in the economy.

A second problem—that of assuring adequate retirement incomes—has also emerged on the horizon. As discussed in Chapter 1, the scheduled rise in the normal retirement age, plus higher projected Medicare premiums and income taxes, will dramatically cut the recipient's net

Social Security benefits. If solvency is restored through a plan that cuts benefits and increases taxes by comparable amounts, it would reduce Social Security replacement rates below their lowest level in the program's history.

Employer plans are not prepared to take on more of the burden. The share of the workforce participating in a plan and the level of contributions have been roughly constant for the past quarter century. But the continuing shift from defined-benefit to defined-contribution plans has placed more of the risks and responsibilities on the shoulders of individual workers, and workers have not demonstrated great success in managing their accounts. Thus, employer plans are unlikely to make up the shortfall created by the scheduled decline in Social Security benefits, let alone any further reductions.

The next three chapters examine reforms enacted in the United Kingdom, Australia, and Canada. Like the United States, these three nations all have Anglo-Saxon retirement income systems, with relatively modest public pension programs and a significant reliance on funded employer plans. Each, however, has incorporated equity investments into its social security program, each along the lines of one of the options defined by the 1994–1996 Social Security Advisory Council. The experiences of these nations thus provide instructive examples of what might play out if we were to adopt one of these three ways forward.

Notes

1. Elderly households are defined as households headed by someone age 65 or older.

2. Although this example uses 65 as the retirement age, the so-called normal retirement age—the age when the worker is eligible for full benefits—is in the process of moving from 65 to 67 by 2022. The increase began with individuals who reached age 62 in 2000, for whom the normal retirement age is 65 plus two months, and increases two months per year until it reaches age 66. Then, after a 12-year hiatus, the normal retirement age begins to increase again by two months per year until it reaches age 67 for individuals who reach 62 in 2022 or later.

3. The Munnell and Soto (2005a) replacement rates presented in Table 3.2 are somewhat different from the hypothetical rates published by the U.S. Social Security Administration (SSA) and presented in Table 3.1. Munnell and Soto give benefits as a percentage of AIME, or average indexed monthly earnings. The SSA hypothetical rates give benefits as a percentage of hypothetical earnings prior to

retirement. For the "medium earner" this is national average earnings when the worker is age 64. The SSA specification of preretirement earnings is somewhat higher than AIME. If the SSA defined preretirement earnings as AIME, the hypothetical "medium" earner would have a 48 percent replacement rate. Conversely, adjusting Munnell and Soto's 44 percent overall rate, for comparability with the SSA figures, would produce a replacement rate somewhat less than the SSA's 42 percent.

4. Especially in collectively bargained plans, the annuity might be a dollar amount per month for each year of service, say $50, so workers with 20 years of service would receive $1,000 per month at age 65.

5. Such plans motivate workers to remain with the firm because benefits based on final earnings increase rapidly as job tenures lengthen. They also encourage workers to retire at an age when productivity typically falls below their compensation. Thus workers who stay past the plan's designated retirement age forgo their pension while they work, with no increase in future benefits. As a result, their net compensation is equal to the difference between their wage and their foregone pension. Considerable work has documented the impact of incentives to retire in defined-benefit plans: Lazear (1979, 1985); Samwick (1998); Stock and Wise (1990a,b); Kotlikoff and Wise (1987, 1989); and Fields and Mitchell (1984).

6. The PBGC monthly guarantee limit in 2005 is $3,801 at age 65 and declines to $1,710 at age 55. Employers pay for this insurance with premiums largely determined by the plan's funding status.

7. In addition to imposing this new funding requirement, Congress dramatically raised PBGC premiums—to $19 plus a "risk adjusted" premium equal to 0.8 percent of the plan's unfunded termination liability—and gave the PBGC a claim against 100 percent of the sponsor's net worth. Many of these changes were enacted in the Omnibus Budget Reconciliation Act of 1987.

8. Nonprofit and governmental organizations have shifted towards 403(b) and 457 plans, which are very similar to 401(k)s. Many large sponsors of defined-benefit plans in the late 1990s were shifting to new hybrid formats, such as the "cash balance plan," that replace the worker's pension benefit with an individual defined-contribution type account. In a cash balance plan, employers contribute the full amount, equal to a set percentage of salary, and increase the balance by a rate of return they set. Like a traditional defined-benefit plan, the assets of the pension fund, the sponsor, and the PBGC all stand behind these balances. As the government clarifies the rules governing cash balance conversions, many large sponsors are expected to adopt this defined-contribution format for their "defined-benefit" program, or to switch to a more conventional 401(k) (Munnell and Sundén 2004).

9. The biggest increase in both absolute and relative costs of defined-benefit versus defined-contribution plans occurred in the late 1980s as plans adjusted to the Retirement Equity Act of 1984 and the Tax Reform Act of 1986 that increased record-keeping requirements, administrative expenses, and benefit costs (Hustead 1998).

10. Retirement incentives have also been reduced in the Social Security program. The 1983 amendments introduced actuarially fair increases in benefits for retirement between the normal retirement age and age 70, to be fully phased in for workers attaining age 62 after 2004. As Social Security early retirement benefits were already actuarially adjusted, the lifetime benefits of a worker with average life expectancy will be about the same regardless of whether benefits are claimed at age 62, 65, or 70 (aside from changes due to additional work). The 1983 amendments also relaxed the Social Security earnings test, and legislation eliminated the earnings test entirely for those who reached the normal retirement age. For a fuller discussion of the evolution of the earnings test and the delayed retirement credit, see DeWitt (1999).

4
Lessons from the United Kingdom
Privatization and a Safety Net

The United Kingdom has included equity investment in its Social Security program along the lines of the "carve-out" individual account approach. The goal of the reform was to restore solvency, reduce dependence on the state, and increase reliance on individual initiative and private financial markets. The United Kingdom achieved solvency by cutting benefits. It then allowed workers to make up the shortfall in projected retirement income by redirecting a portion of their social insurance contributions to an individual account, which could be invested in equities. The recent withdrawal of many employers from offering traditional defined-benefit pensions, which could also substitute for a portion of the government pension program, has made an individual account the primary choice for workers electing the carve-out option.

Britain's individual account program, however, has been hampered by high administrative costs and governance challenges that market forces have thus far been unable to bring under control. Benefits provided by the Basic State Pension have meanwhile fallen below 15 percent of national average earnings and are projected to hit 7 percent midcentury. Because welfare benefits are pegged at 20 percent of national average earnings, and because Britain introduced a "tapered" withdrawal rate for old-age means-tested benefits, reducing benefits by only a percentage of income earned, half the elderly are now eligible for welfare benefits. By mid-century this figure is projected to be three-quarters of the elderly, with a greater proportion on means-tested benefits at some point in their lives. Thus, the carve-out approach in Britain is expected to change the public retirement system from social insurance to one increasingly based on means-tested welfare benefits.

THE UK RETIREMENT SYSTEM IN 1980

Through the early postwar decades, the United Kingdom had a standard two-tier Anglo-Saxon retirement income system. The first tier was the Basic State Pension, a social insurance program funded by a payroll tax, which had evolved out of the nation's 1908 means-tested welfare program for the elderly. The Basic State Pension provided full-career workers a "basic pension," which was kept at about 20 percent of national average earnings through the first three postwar decades (Figure 4.1). The second tier was the collection of tax-advantaged employer plans, which provided earnings replacement for workers who remained with their employers to retirement. Half the wage and salary workforce, and two-thirds of the men, were covered by such a plan at the end of the 1970s. But, as indicated by the elderly's heavy dependence on the government's meager old-age benefits, only a small number of retirees at the time had an adequate income from an employer plan (Figure 4.2).

Figure 4.1 UK's Basic State Pension as a Percent of National Average Earnings, 1950–2005

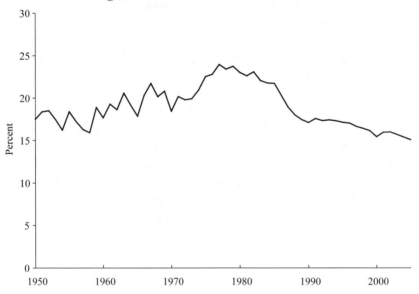

SOURCE: UK Government Actuary (2003).

Figure 4.2 Sources of Retirement Income in the United Kingdom and the United States, 1979

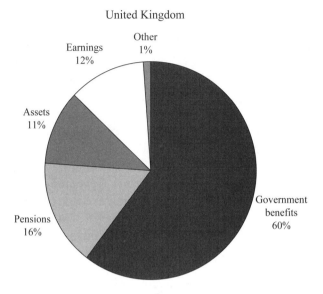

United Kingdom

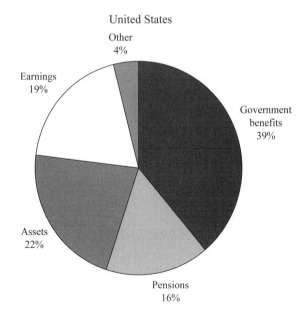

United States

SOURCE: Davis (1997); Federal Interagency Forum on Aging-Related Statistics (2004).

Like the United States, the United Kingdom expanded its retirement income system in the 1970s in response to two distinct problems—the persistence of old-age poverty and the sharp drop in income that most workers experienced when they retired from the labor force. Parliament addressed the problem of old-age poverty in 1975 by expanding the Basic State Pension. It pushed benefits to 25 percent of the national wage. It also gave the disabled and those who remained at home to care for young children or other family members (primarily married women) credit toward benefits. These reforms made the Basic State Pension less of an employment-based social insurance program and more of a demogrant—a uniform payment made to a group of residents—which improved its success in keeping the elderly out of poverty.

Parliament addressed the problem of income maintenance by strengthening the earnings-related second tier of the nation's retirement income system. In 1973, it imposed a five-year vesting requirement on employer plans.[1] Many more workers could thus expect to retire with at least some earnings-related retirement income. Parliament's major income-maintenance initiative, however, was the creation of the State Earnings Related Pension Scheme (SERPS). Enacted in 1975 and going into effect in 1978, the new SERPS program was scheduled to replace 25 percent of earnings between the level of the Basic State Pension (then 25 percent of average earnings) and 7.5 times that amount (then a bit below twice average earnings).

The addition of this earnings-related old-age pension changed the structure of the British social insurance program, making it more like the U.S. Social Security program. Once SERPS matured, in 20 years, the "average earner" would get a combined Basic State Pension/SERPS pension replacing nearly 44 percent of preretirement earnings: 25 percent from the Basic State Pension and nearly 19 percent (25 percent of earnings above the Basic State Pension) from SERPS. The U.S. Social Security program has a similar structure. For a worker with average earnings, Social Security replaces 90 percent of the first 22 percent of the worker's average indexed earnings and 32 percent of earnings above that amount (Table 4.1). This yields a replacement rate of 45 percent of average indexed earnings. Such two-tier pension packages provide higher benefits to high earners, who contribute more, and lower benefits to low earners, who contribute less, but they replace more of the low earner's wage to assure a minimum old-age income.[2]

Table 4.1 The Structure of U.S. and UK Social Security Systems after the 1978 Reforms

Hypothetical social security replacement rate (%) for the average worker

U.S. system[a]		UK System	
90% portion of the benefit formula	20	Basic State Pension	25
32% portion of the benefit formula	25	SERPS	19
Total replacement	45	Total replacement	44

[a] The U.S. replacement rates presented in this table are Social Security benefits as a percent of average indexed earnings, using the benefit formula presented in Table 3.1.
SOURCE: Authors' calculations.

The fundamental difference between the expanded British and U.S. Social Security programs was the ability of British employers to "contract out" of SERPS. Employers that offered comparable benefits—to both leavers and stayers—were in fact encouraged to "contract out." The government provided that encouragement by giving employers that contract out a "rebate" of the payroll tax that funded SERPS. This rebate was set somewhat above the estimated cost of the benefit.[3] SERPS was thus a residual program, designed for those not covered by an employer plan. It also served as a benchmark that defined the minimum earnings-related benefit for workers covered by employer plans. At the end of the 1970s, 53 percent of workers eligible for SERPS were contracted out, leaving just 47 percent contributing to the government program (Davis 1997; Whitehouse 1998).

The ability to contract out meant that employer plans in the United Kingdom would play a larger role than they do in the United States. The plans that contracted out, and most did, would provide the second tier of the public pension benefit. They would also supplement public benefits to replace the earnings of career employees, as they did in the United States.

Aside from this ability for employers to contract out, the United States and the United Kingdom had similar retirement income systems at the end of the 1970s. The expanded UK public pension program was designed to replace about 44 percent of the "average worker's" earnings, essentially the same as Social Security. Both countries also had broad participation in tax-advantaged employer defined-benefit pension plans, and these plans then provided about 16 percent of the income of the elderly (Figure 4.3). Both countries also had adopted vesting

Figure 4.3 Projections of UK Public Pension Benefits as a Percent of Average Earnings, 1979–2060

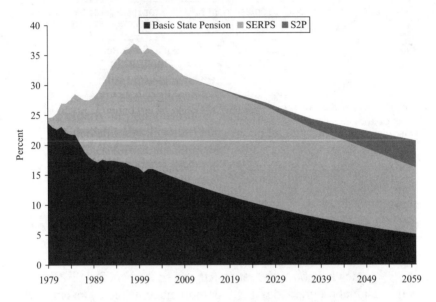

NOTE: S2P is the State Second Pension, a replacement for SERPS introduced in 2002 that provides higher benefits for low-wage workers and SERPS-level benefits for workers with middle and high earnings.
SOURCE: UK Government Actuary (2003).

requirements designed to provide retirement income benefits to a far greater share of the workforce.

The two nations responded quite differently to challenges that emerged at the end of the twentieth century. Britain was quick to adopt the carve-out response. More than any other industrial nation, it cut government pensions and shifted much of the responsibility of providing the diminished level of public benefits to the private sector.[4] Its experience thus illustrates possible implications of such policies for the United States.

THE REFORM OF THE BRITISH RETIREMENT INCOME SYSTEM: CONTRACTION AND PRIVATIZATION

The government-led expansion of the British retirement income system proved short lived. In 1979, only one year after the new SERPS program went into effect, the Conservatives under Margaret Thatcher came to power and remained in office for the next 18 years. Thatcher was elected on a platform that promised to privatize and deregulate the economy, cut social spending, reduce the power of unions, and lower the overall tax burden. The National Insurance Contribution payroll tax that funded government old-age pensions, as well as other social programs, took about 15 percent of covered earnings. It was a major component of overall taxation, especially for low and middle earners. Reputable studies also began projecting a rapid aging of the population, a sharp increase in pension expenditures, and payroll tax rates rising to 35 percent of covered earnings after 2010 (Whitehouse 1998). Controlling public expenditures on old-age pensions thus became a major policy objective. As private plans were funded in advance and had a strong voluntary component, they promised a smoother and less costly transition to an older society. The fiscal implications of societal aging and the perceived advantages of private plans thus intensified the Conservative impulse to pare down social insurance and privatize the retirement income system (UK Department for Work and Pensions 2000).

The campaign began in 1980, when the Conservatives indexed the Basic State Pension to prices rather than wages. As wages typically rise faster than prices, the change in indexing meant that the program would require an ever smaller share of earnings and national output as compared to the pre-1980 policy. It also set Basic State Pension benefits on a slow but steady path of replacing an ever-smaller share of preretirement earnings. By the beginning of the twenty-first century, benefits would fall from 25 to 15 percent of national average earnings. The Basic State Pension is projected to replace 10 percent of national average earnings by 2030, and just 7 percent by midcentury (UK Government Actuary 2003).

The Conservatives turned to the earnings-related portion of the public retirement income system in 1986 and 1995. They cut the SERPS pension from 25 percent of the average of a worker's best 20 years of covered earnings to 20 percent of average covered earnings over the worker's full career, reduced the amount of earnings covered by the program, halved the survivor benefit from 100 to 50 percent of the deceased spouse's benefit, increased the retirement age for women from 60 to 65, and introduced various technical procedures that further reduced SERPS pensions. The changes would cut the benefits to just a quarter of their original 1978 level, with married women bearing a disproportionate share of the reduction (Blake 2000; Davis 1997; Hannah 1986; Nobles 2000; UK Department for Work and Pensions 2000; Whitehouse 1998).

As the Conservatives reduced social insurance pensions, they shifted more of the retirement income burden to private plans. They would require vesting after two years of service, pension fund assets sufficient to meet at least 90 percent of the plan's current obligations, a stricter standard of fiduciary conduct, and participation in an "insurance" pool that protected participants against fraud.[5] In addition to these ERISA-like rules, the Conservatives would also require employers to index both vested accruals and pension benefits to inflation of up to 5 percent per year (Blake 2000, 2002; Davis 1997; Hannah 1986; Nobles 2000; UK Department for Work and Pensions 2000; Whitehouse 1998).

The privatization campaign was stymied, however, by the stagnation in employer plan coverage. Coverage in fact had peaked in 1967 and was slowly trending down (Davis 2003). As in the United States, production was shifting away from the traditional pension sponsors—large hierarchic enterprises and unionized industries—toward smaller firms and employers of the rapidly growing supply of women and mobile knowledge workers. Defined-contribution plans were far better suited than defined-benefit pension plans to smaller firms and workers with multiple-employer careers. To expand the reach of private plans—and to create a more fluid, noncorporate, non-union, and market-driven economy—the Conservatives promoted the growth of individual account retirement plans (Davis 1997; Nobles 2000).

Beginning in 1986, the government allowed firms and workers to contract out of SERPS using "money purchase" plans, individual retirement savings accounts that annuitized the balance at retirement.[6] These money purchase plans could either be individual "personal pension" policies offered by insurers or employer-sponsored money purchase plans. To accelerate the adoption of personal pensions, the Conservatives between 1988 and 1993 offered a higher "rebate" of social insurance contributions to workers who took out such plans—an additional 2 percent of covered earnings atop the 5.8 percent rebate then given for workers that were contracted out through a traditional employer defined-benefit plan. They also allowed workers to opt out of their employer defined-benefit plan and direct the standard payroll tax rebate, and this 2 percent bonus, to a personal pension. They even allowed workers to cash-out the value of their defined-benefit plan accrual and deposit the sum into a personal pension (Davis 1997; Daykin 2001).

The government's promotion of private pensions succeeded in boosting the number of workers that were contracted out of SERPS into some sort of prefunded private retirement plan (see Figure 4.4). The spread of individual retirement savings account plans was never-

Figure 4.4 Percent of All UK Workers Covered by Employer Plans or Personal Pensions, 1979–2002

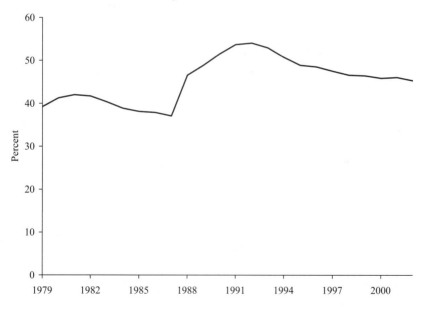

NOTE: Coverage includes both public and private sector wage and salary workers. The coverage rates thus are not strictly comparable to those for the United States presented in Figure 2.2, which includes only private sector workers.
SOURCE: UK Department for Work and Pensions (2003b).

theless slower in Britain than in the United States. The additional 2 percent rebate primarily led to a shift out of SERPS, more than out of employer defined-benefit plans (Table 4.2). SERPS, as a result, covered less than 40 percent of workers in second-tier earnings-related plans by the end of the 1980s. The growth of individual retirement savings accounts thereafter came mainly at the expense of employer defined-benefit plans. By the mid-1990s, 80 percent of new employer plans had a defined-contribution format, a rate similar to that in the United States, and over a third of all workers in private plans were in an individual account arrangement (Whitehouse 1998). The pace of structural economic change, firm creation, and new plan formation nevertheless proceeded at a slower pace in Britain. So employer defined-benefit plans remained the dominant private retirement income vehicle through the end of the twentieth century.

In 1997, the Conservatives made a bold attempt to completely privatize the retirement income system. They proposed the replacement of both the Basic State Pension and SERPS by mandatory participation in a private plan—presumably an individual account for those not already contracted out—with a minimum contribution equal to 9 percent of earnings. The Conservatives argued that such a plan was the key to raising the old-age incomes of those at the bottom. They saw employer plans as a financial vehicle giving middle- and upper-income workers access to the capital markets and high-yielding equity investments, which would allow the conversion of current earnings into ample old-age pensions. A key hurdle impeding access to the capital markets by low-wage workers was the fixed setup and marketing costs of personal pension accounts, which took a large bite out of the contributions and investment returns of low and middle earners. One study estimated an

Table 4.2 Coverage in the United Kingdom by Type of Plan for Those with Earnings-Related Pensions

Type of plan	Coverage (%)			
	1978–79	1987–88	1994–95	2001–02
Employer defined-benefit plan	51	46	40	35
Money purchase plan	0	16	24	20
SERPS	49	38	36	45

SOURCE: UK Department for Work and Pensions (2003b).

average reduction of 3.2 percentage points in annual returns for participation over a 10-year period and 1.7 percentage points for a 25-year period. Another found fees and high turnover rates often reduced the value of individual account balances of low-wage workers by 40 percent or more. By raising the guaranteed contribution to 9 percent of covered earnings, approximately twice the level of the payroll tax rebate, the overhead burden could be cut roughly in half. As a fail-safe against the risks inherent in such plans, the Conservatives would also guarantee an income at least equal to the Basic State Pension on the "first-tier" portion of the mandatory contribution (Blake and Board 2000; Davis 1997; Murthi, Orszag, and Orszag 1999; Whitehouse 1998).

The Conservative privatization campaign and proposal to eliminate public old-age pensions came to an end in the election of 1997. Labor made retirement income policy a major campaign issue, and the resulting debate contributed to the Conservatives' worst defeat since 1832.[7] Labor did not, however, reverse the basic privatization approach. It declared its ambition that private plans would provide 60 percent of retirement income by the middle of the twenty-first century and that the great majority of the elderly would get at least some support from private sources. But Labor developed alternate approaches for including low and middle earners in private plans and for assuring a minimal retirement income (Whitehouse 1998).

THE REFORM OF THE BRITISH RETIREMENT INCOME SYSTEM: PRIVATIZATION WITH A SAFETY NET

Labor recognized that the overhead costs of personal pensions were a significant problem for low and middle earners, with their low level of contributions and low account balances. So, in 2001, Labor introduced the "Stakeholder pension," effectively a personal pension with fees limited to 1 percent of assets and with no charges for initiating or exiting an account.[8] The government also required employers without their own plans to offer their workers a Stakeholder option. By imposing this requirement, controlling fees, and sanctioning the design, the government hoped to accelerate the acceptance of Stakeholder pensions. This was especially important as the low-fee accounts required enormous economies of scale to be commercially viable (UK Department for Work and Pensions 1998; 2002a).

The Stakeholder design limited the overhead burden by fiat, but it remained costly for financial services firms to market and administer such plans, especially for workers with low contributions and balances. Advising low and middle earners whether or not to contract out and how best to allocate their assets in a retirement plan was also expensive. Should these firms give erroneous advice, they risked being accused of mis-selling and facing stiff financial penalties. Because of these very real costs and risks, financial services firms have not aggressively pursued Stakeholder business and take-up has been disappointing. In response, the government in 2004 increased allowable fees to 1.5 percent of assets over the first 10 years of contributions. Even at this level, observers question whether fees could cover costs in the low- to average-earner market. A 1.5 percent fee also represents a major reduction in investment earnings, resulting in about a 30 percent reduction in assets at retirement if maintained across the entire accumulation period (Blake and Turner 2005; UK Pensions Commission 2005).

Labor's most significant reforms addressed the problem of assuring the elderly a basic income—the issue that had initiated the rise of modern retirement income systems. Because of Britain's meager social insurance program and the limited reach of private plans, one out of six elderly Britons in the 1990s collected national means-tested cash payments.[9] With the contraction of social insurance, the issue of assuring the elderly a basic income required a serious policy response.

The most obvious approach would be to restore the Basic State Pension to its traditional peg of about 20 percent of average earnings. Restoring the Basic State Pension, however, would increase benefits to all retirees, not just those in poverty. To keep a lid on public expenditures, Labor continued the policy of price-indexing the Basic State Pension, which produces a steady decline in benefits relative to earnings.

To augment public pensions for low and middle earners, Labor increased their benefits in the government's second-tier earnings-related program. In 2002, Labor replaced SERPS with the State Second Pension. This new program broke the direct relationship between benefits and earnings to increase pensions of those at the bottom. After the program was fully phased in:

- Full career workers with earnings of about 45 percent of national average earnings would receive 40 percent of covered earnings.

- Workers with less than 45 percent of national average earnings would receive the same amount as the 45 percent earner.

- Workers with earnings above 45 percent of national average earnings would receive a higher benefit, but the amount of preretirement earnings replaced would decline as earnings rose until reaching the SERPS 20 percent replacement rate.

Thus, the benefits provided by the State Second Pension were a flat amount at the bottom of the income distribution, gently sloped in the middle, and proportional to earnings only at levels where most workers contract out. The new system would thus function more like the welfare-derived Basic State Pension, assuring a minimal income, than the market-derived SERPS, with benefits proportional to contributions. Labor also provided caregivers and the disabled credit toward a second-tier pension, which represented another shift toward a welfare-based model. The combination of the Basic State Pension and the State Second Pension still gave higher earners higher social insurance pensions, but benefits would not be much greater than those going to workers with much lower earnings.[10]

Even for low earners, however, the larger benefits provided by the State Second Pension will only partially offset the decline of the Basic State Pension. Public pensions are thus expected to replace a steadily declining share of preretirement earnings. One estimate has the combined pension falling to 28 percent of national average earnings for the average earner as early as 2025 and to 21 percent—Britain's traditional welfare-level allowance—for those earning half the national average earnings (Pensions Policy Institute 2003). Labor's social insurance reforms thus targeted the government's scarce resources on those at the bottom. It preserved the basic welfare-level pension for low earners without private coverage, and it left those in private plans with just the dwindling Basic State Pension (Pensions Policy Institute 2003).

Labor's most far-reaching reform was the addition of the "pension credit" to the nation's means-tested welfare program for the elderly in 2003. The nation's welfare program had traditionally reduced means-tested benefits pound for pound once the recipient's total income crossed the targeted threshold amount, which was about 20 percent of national average earnings in the postwar period. As the Basic State Pension falls below that target, an increasing proportion of the elderly would see income earned through work, savings, or contributions to public or private retirement plans merely reduce their means-tested benefits on a pound-for-pound basis.[11] The pension credit cut that confiscatory tax to a more manageable 40 percent. That is, after the application of the pension credit, a pound of income above the Basic State Pension lowers means-tested benefits by 40 pence. This tapered withdrawal of means-tested benefits reduced the sense of unfairness, and the draconian disincentive to work or save, that the traditional approach would impose on an increasing share of the elderly as the Basic State Pension declined (Clark 2001, 2002; Clark and Emmerson 2003).

At the same time, the pension credit taper significantly increased the share of the elderly that qualifies for means-tested payments. Before the introduction of the program, retirees with a full Basic State Pension (about 15 percent of national average earnings in 2003) lost all means-tested benefits if they had income from other sources greater than 5 percent of national average earnings. With the pension credit, retirees with other income up to 13 percent of national average earnings—about half the elderly—qualify for a benefit. When the Basic State Pension reaches 10 percent of national average earnings, retirees with other income up to 25 percent of national average earnings would qualify (Pensions Policy Institute 2003). Estimates of the eligible population by mid-century, with a Basic State Pension estimated at 7 percent of national average earnings, range from 65 to 80 percent of the elderly (Figure 4.5). The great majority of British households would thus be eligible for means-tested benefits—if not at the time of retirement, then later in life, as old-age incomes typically decline over time, especially relative to national average earnings (Clark and Emmerson 2002, 2003; Pensions Policy Institute 2003; UK Department for Work and Pensions 2002b).[12]

AN ASSESSMENT OF THE REFORMED BRITISH SYSTEM

The British responded to the demographic and economic challenges that emerged after 1980 as aggressively as any advanced industrial na-

Figure 4.5 Projected Percentage of UK Pensioners Eligible for Pension Credit

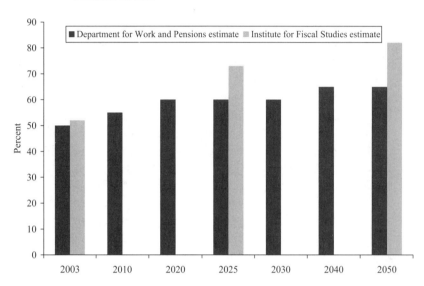

SOURCE: Pensions Policy Institute (2003).

tion. The British system at the beginning of the period looked much like that in the United States, with social insurance and employer defined-benefit plans promising reasonably ample incomes to much of the elderly population. By the end of the period, the roles of both social insurance and employer defined-benefit plans had been greatly diminished. If the current system remains in place, three out of four elderly Britons will rely on means-tested benefits by the middle of the twenty-first century and individual accounts will be the primary source of private retirement income.

A key public policy objective throughout was to reduce the pressure on government budgets, and ease the transition to an older society, by privatizing much of the retirement income burden. This objective has largely been realized. In a world in which nearly all industrial nations face enormous public pension obligations, Britain is widely admired for containing government expenditures on the elderly to about 5 percent of GDP. Social insurance spending is projected to fall by midcentury, from a bit more than 4 percent of GDP today to a bit more than 3 percent, with the erosion of the Basic State Pension and the rising retirement age for women more than offsetting the effects of population aging (UK Pension Commission 2004). These cuts will help contain payroll tax rates, which fund the National Health Service as well as old-age pensions. Meanwhile means-tested expenditures, paid out of general revenues, are projected to rise from less than 0.5 to over 1 percent of GDP over this period (Clark 2001, 2002; Davis 2003; UK Department for Work and Pensions 2003a).

Britain's privatization initiative required employer plans to assume an increasing share of the retirement income burden. In this, however, Britain has been far less successful. Employer defined-benefit plans faced similar demographic and economic forces as they did in the United States, but their burdens were greater, because they typically contracted out the government's second-tier pension and the government imposed increasingly stringent inflation-proofing requirements on employer plan accruals and benefit payouts. The boom of the 1980s and 1990s lightened the burden, but the economic downturn at the turn of the century resulted in major employer plan deficits. By year-end 2002, assets averaged just 80 percent of liabilities in the plans of Britain's 100 largest firms (Davis 2003). In some cases the deficit exceeded 40 percent of the sponsor's market value. As in the United States, new government funding rules required a sharp increase in pension contributions to quickly fund termination liabilities—just when the sponsor's business was struggling. Employers could also see that defined-benefit plans would remain a costly affair even after the recession ended. In response, employers with half of all private-sector defined-benefit participants have closed their plans to new entrants (Davis 2003). Government agencies and enterprises have retained their defined-benefit programs, but retirement saving in the British private sector, as in the United States, will increasingly be organized around individual accounts.[13]

Given the continued erosion of government pensions and the decline in employer defined-benefit plans, individual accounts have emerged as critically important in the British retirement income system. The challenge of retirement income planning is much the same in individual accounts and employer defined-benefit plans. There is a need to adequately fund the plan, invest the assets, manage the risks, generate the desired income stream, and seek out qualified vendors and advisors. Employers bring tremendous sophistication to the task. Workers bring little or none, nor does the British experience suggest that workers become more sophisticated as government and employer benefits decline, although the stakes become significantly greater.

The clearest indication of this lack of proper management is the low level of contributions to individual accounts. Contributions to employer defined-benefit plans, largely determined by actuarial analysis, run about 16 percent of payroll. This is larger than contributions in the United States, as British plans generally contract out and take on the burden of paying public second-tier pension benefits to terminated as well as active workers and are required to provide significant levels of inflation-proofing. By contrast, the average contribution to defined-contribution plans is half that amount—8.5 percent of earnings in employer plans and only 7.7 percent of earnings in the far more prevalent personal pensions (Davis 2003). Under some circumstances, this level of contribution could produce a reasonable balance at retirement. British private pensions, however, have very high overhead costs, which reduce the ultimate accumulation. Contribution rates, moreover, are not constant across a worker's career. Government rebates of social insurance contributions for workers in defined-contribution plans rise sharply with age. They start at 5 percent of covered earnings and rise to 13 percent of covered earnings for workers age 52 and over. The large contributions made toward the end of a worker's career, however, have relatively little impact on the account balance at retirement. This back-loaded pattern of contributions, combined with higher overhead costs, is unlikely to produce an adequate retirement income (Blake 2002; Davis 1997, 2003; UK Department of Work and Pension 2002; Whitehouse 1998).

Older workers also have not been very effective in translating their account balances into retirement income streams. Until April 2006, the government required the annuitization of balances created by payroll tax rebates, with payments increasing at least 3 percent per annum as a protection against expected inflation.[14] In fulfilling this requirement, workers commonly failed to shop around for the best value. Even when other providers offered far more retirement income in exchange for their balances, retiring workers often annuitized with the firm that had managed the accumulation phase. Most workers also choose not to annuitize their nonpayroll tax balances. Such decisions create a significant risk of insufficient income down the road (Davis 1997, 2003).

The lack of proper management is most dramatically illustrated in the "mis-selling" scandal that erupted in 1993. Workers had been given the right to contract out of SERPS or their employer plan using a personal pension in 1986. Encouraged by commission-driven insurance agents, millions of workers contracted out of SERPS and 500,000 out of employer defined-benefit plans. Some of the former, and most of the latter, made a serious financial error. Workers in their mid-40s or over were generally better off in SERPS, let alone in far more generous employer defined-benefit plans.[15] Opting out of an employer plan typically meant the loss of the employer's pension contribution, ancillary disability and life insurance benefits, and the plan's risk pooling and administrative economies.[16] Workers dissatisfied with their particular provider, or unable to continue contributing at the initial agreed-upon rate, would also discover that most plans had very low cash values in the early years of the program, as a large portion of their contributions went to pay commissions and set-up fees (Blake 2000, 2002; Davis 1997, 2000; Murthi, Orszag, and Orszag 1999).

The scandal resulted in the insurance industry paying an estimated 11 billion British pounds (GBP) as compensation to mis-sold workers (Davis 2000). It also produced tougher controls on both the financial services industry and individual decision making. Personal pension providers must now disclose commissions and surrender values over the first five years of the contract. To transfer accruals in employer defined-benefit plans to a personal pension, workers now need a written explanation, prepared by a trained expert and checked by the insurer, demonstrating the gain. These reforms responded to specific lapses but fail to address the larger management problem—the complexity of retirement income decision making, the inability of workers to make proper decisions, and the asymmetric nature of the financial services market—where customers lack the knowledge and information needed to properly evaluate offers prepared by sophisticated vendors. This larger problem drives up costs, generates confusion and mistrust, creates opportunities for gaming, mis-selling, and error, and significantly reduces the overall efficiency of the retirement income system (Blake 2000, 2002; Davis 2000; Emmerson 2002; Whitehouse 1998).

Overhead costs also remain a serious impediment. Britain's individual accounts have largely been organized as "retail" personal pensions, rather than delivered "wholesale" through employers, as are U.S.

401(k) plans. The Conservatives had hoped that market competition and/or higher contributions would drive down fees and charges, but competition has not significantly lowered the price of personal pensions. Labor had hoped to lower costs by introducing the Stakeholder pension, with its strictly capped fees, but financial services firms have not aggressively pursued Stakeholder business. Given the maximum fees and charges, they view the prospect of a mass-market take-up, large economies of scale, and long-run profitability as too chancy to justify entry. Marketing and administering individual accounts thus remains a costly endeavor, limiting their ability to generate retirement income for low and middle earners.

CONCLUSION

The success of Britain's retirement income policy required that employer plans expand to offset the cuts in social insurance. Initiatives to enhance the contribution of employer defined-benefit plans—especially the imposition of inflation-proofing and tougher funding rules—have generally had the opposite effect. The use of individual accounts to expand the reach of employer plans—especially among low and middle earners—has met with limited success at best. And the shift from defined-benefit to defined-contribution arrangements will likely reduce the overall contribution of private plans.

Britain's current safety net, if it remains in place, will guarantee the elderly an income of about 20 percent of national average earnings— the traditional welfare stipend. The pension credit should lift most of the elderly above this minimal income floor. But because of the contraction of public and private pensions, most workers will see a significant decline in their standard of living in retirement. In 2050, three out of four are projected to qualify for means-tested pension credit benefits. With the Basic State Pension at a projected 7 percent of national average earnings, 75 percent of the elderly would have incomes less than 40 percent of national average earnings. A recent British study found that such a standard was "modest but adequate" (Parker 2002). While significantly less than the income needed to maintain preretirement living standards, it does afford "full opportunity to participate in contemporary society and the basic options it offers." In 2050, however, the great majority of the elderly would *at best* have incomes that provide this basic level of social participation (Clark and Emmerson 2002; Liu 1999; Parker 2002; Pensions Policy Institute 2003; UK Department of Work and Pensions 2002b).

This general dependence on means-tested benefits threatens to change the character of the retirement income system and thereby the lives of the elderly. It could diminish the dignity of recipients, create disincentives to work or save, and generate conflicts between those receiving means-tested benefits and those paying the bill. It was precisely this general dependence and these adverse effects that led Britain, like other industrial nations, to replace its means-tested program for the elderly with social insurance pensions. But Britain's decision to sharply cut its social insurance programs and increase reliance on individual initiatives has returned the nation to a welfare-based solution to the old-age income problem.[17]

Notes

1. The law went into effect in 1975; in 1985, Parliament required vesting after two years of service (Blake and Orszag 1997; UK Department for Work and Pensions 2000).
2. The hypothetical replacement rates reported by the Social Security Administration and presented in Table 3.1 are calculated on a somewhat different basis and produce a 42 percent replacement rate for the average earner. See Box 3.1 (p. 46) for a more detailed description of the Social Security benefit formula.
3. The estimate included administrative expenses, which increased costs above the government alternative. But the estimate assumed a significant use of equities in funding the benefit, which reduced the rebate far below the present value of the future pension benefit discounted at the riskless government bond rate. The rebate given to employer defined-benefit plans for workers contracted out of SERPS is reset periodically and as a percentage of covered earnings has been: 7 percent (1978–1983); 6.25 percent (1983–1988); 5.8 percent (1988–1993); 4.8 percent (1993–1997); 4.6 percent (1997–2002); and 5.1 percent (2002–2007) (Daykin 2001).
4. The carve-out approach 1) restores solvency by cutting benefits, and 2) allows workers to carve a contribution to a private retirement plan out of the payroll tax in exchange for a reduction in their future Social Security benefits. In the United Kingdom, the ability to "contract out" of SERPS means that "carving out" a contribution to a private retirement plan was an integral feature of the expanded UK

system, not a response to demographic and economic challenges that emerged after 1980.

5. Earlier rules required actuarial certification of assets sufficient to pay only the contracted-out benefit.

6. On balances created by payroll tax rebates, at least three-quarters had to be annuitized using unisex rates, with payments rising at least 3 percent per annum to accommodate expected inflation and with spouses getting at least a 50 percent survivor benefit.

7. A Conservative proposal to change the taxation of private plans—their response to the financing crisis created by the privatization of pay-as-you-go social insurance—emerged as a key election issue. Privatization would eliminate both the social insurance revenue stream and the accrual of further social insurance obligations. But the government still had to honor pensions and benefits accrued in the past. To pay these pensions, the Conservatives would bring the taxation of pensions forward. They would eliminate the deductibility of current contributions and make future benefits tax-exempt. While this did not cover the entire liability, the remaining burden became manageable. Labor, however, hammered away at this loss of deductibility and emphasized the political risk, inherent in such proposals, that future governments would reimpose a tax on retirement benefits.

8. Providers could also require no more than £20 to open a Stakeholder account.

9. One-third of the elderly received means-tested benefits from either the local or national government (Pensions Policy Institute 2003).

10. The government expected 18 million workers to benefit from the new program: 5 million low earners at the 40 percent accrual rate, mainly part-time women workers; 9 million middle earners; 2 million caregivers; and 2 million disabled (UK Department for Work and Pensions 1998, 2000). For details on the program, see Sass (2003).

11. Income from accumulated savings is not the actual income generated, but "deemed" at £1 of income for every £500 of savings over £6,000 (UK Department for Work and Pensions 2003a). The means test typically ignored the first few pounds of earnings—the first £5 for individuals and £10 for couples (Clark and Emmerson 2003).

12. The two estimates differ largely because of differences in projections of annual real earnings growth (2 percent versus 1.5 percent) and whether the elderly are defined as the population age 65 and older or age 60 and older.

13. The Finance Act of 1986, enacted at a time of serious budgetary pressure, allowed plans to be at most 5 percent overfunded. So rather than build up surpluses during the boom years of the 1980s and 1990s, sponsors took "funding holidays," reducing contributions from 2.7 to 1.2 percent of GDP between 1980 and 1992, and used "excess" assets to sweeten early retirement benefits (Blake 2002; Davis 1997, 2003). As in the United States, the new accounting rules required sponsors to report in their financial statements the pension plan deficits that emerged in the new century.

14. Since April 2006, individuals that do not annuitize by age 75 must take an Alternative Secured Income, which allows for bequests, subjects savings to taxation, and restricts the amounts drawn down to assure a continuing income (HM Revenue and Customs 2004).

15. In employer defined-benefit plans, accruals at the end of a worker's career have the greatest impact on retirement income. SERPS rewards each year more equally. In personal pensions, contributions in the early years of a worker's career have by far the greatest impact. Thus, young workers who contracted out of SERPS—and young workers were the majority of those who did so—made a reasonable financial decision.

16. Some workers opted out of an employer plan to increase their take-home pay. They contributed just the payroll tax rebate to their personal pension and pocketed their former contribution to the employer plan. Such decisions could reflect tremendous liquidity constraints, a low value placed on their own future well-being, or simple financial ignorance.

17. A government Pensions Commission, created in 2002 and headed by Lord Alistair Turner, conducted an exhaustive review of the nation's retirement income system and in 2005 delivered a set of policy recommendations (Pensions Commission 2004, 2005). The Turner Commission proposed a thorough revamping of the British system, including an end of the carve-out approach. It would 1) provide a flat public pension, set at about 30 percent of average earnings, and delivered to all elderly citizens, regardless of employment and contribution history, to fulfill the government's objective of assuring a minimal old-age income with minimal means-testing; 2) raise the age of eligibility for public pensions to 67 by 2040, to control costs and focus resources where they were needed most; and 3) introduce a system of individual accounts, with contributions from workers (4 percent of covered earnings), employers (3 percent of covered earnings), and government (1 percent of covered earnings). The plan would use government administration to reduce recordkeeping overhead and private asset management. Workers would be automatically enrolled in the plan but allowed to opt out. For the "average earner" who participates, the combined system would produce an estimated 45 percent replacement rate. As of the completion of this manuscript, the government has taken no action in response to the Turner Commission recommendations.

5
Lessons from Australia
Mandating "Add-On" Individual Accounts

Australia introduced equity investments into its Social Security program along the lines of the "add-on" individual retirement account approach. The analogy is not perfect. The mandatory contributions to Australia's individual accounts, which were introduced in the 1990s, are much larger than those in U.S. add-on proposals. Australia's public retirement income program, moreover, has always been its means-tested Age Pension. Australia never had a social insurance pension plan. The Age Pension was expanded in the 1970s and now guarantees an income equal to about a third of average earnings—far more than the income guaranteed by the UK means-tested program but far less than the pension Social Security provides the "average earner." The combination of the Age Pension and Australia's substantial individual accounts should nevertheless deliver adequate retirement incomes to the nation's elderly population. The Age Pension also performs valuable risk-management service to an elderly population reliant on individual accounts invested in equities. It assures an income to those who outlive their individual account assets, invest poorly, or are in unlucky cohorts when it comes to investment returns.

Using the means-tested Age Pension to cushion the risk in equity investments, however, creates two types of costs. The first is overinvestment in assets that dodge the means test, such as housing, consumer durables, and exotic annuity products created by the financial services industry. Such assets have lower returns than many alternate investments but higher returns after netting out tax and Age Pension reductions. The second cost is an incentive to retire early, spend down individual account assets, and increase reliance on the means-tested Age Pension. To the extent that workers retire early, cut back on saving, or spend down their assets prior to reaching old age, they increase the burden on the system while reducing their retirement incomes.

THE AUSTRALIAN AGE PENSION AT THE END OF
THE 1980s

Australia has by far the most experience of any industrial nation with a retirement income system made up of earnings-based individual accounts and means-tested public pensions. Both Australian programs are also far more substantial than those in the United Kingdom. Australia's experience thus illustrates the importance of size in retirement income planning and also provides insight on potential problems created by the interplay of individual accounts and a generous means-tested program.

Australia's public Age Pension program was introduced in 1908. Like most programs created at the time, it provided a welfare-level allowance to elderly individuals who satisfied a stringent means test. Unlike other nations with such programs, Australia never switched over to social insurance. The means-tested Age Pension remains to this day the nation's first-tier retirement income program. Australia also has a long tradition of employer-provided pensions. From the nineteenth century forward, workers in government and large corporations have been covered by defined-benefit plans.

Like other Anglo-Saxon nations, Australia expanded its retirement income system in the 1970s. It raised the Age Pension allowance from about 20 percent to about 25 percent of "male total average weekly earnings" (see Figure 5.1). It also extended coverage to a much larger portion of the elderly by adding a "taper" to the withdrawal of benefits. Instead of reducing benefits dollar for dollar for income above the "free area"—the income exempt from the Age Pension means test—the government lowered the reduction rate to 40 cents on the dollar. These initiatives significantly changed the character of the Age Pension. Essentially all workers would now get at least some income from the program, and the income was reasonably substantial.

Focusing on male earnings understates the generosity of Age Pension benefits. A large number of women, who earned less on average than men, entered the labor force after 1970 and brought median earnings for the entire workforce to about 75 percent of men's average earnings. The Age Pension, pegged at 25 percent of men's average earnings, thus replaces about 33 percent of the median worker's earnings. This

Figure 5.1 Australian Age Pension Relative to Average Male Earnings, 1965–1999

SOURCE: Commonwealth Treasury of Australia (2001).

makes Australia's Age Pension benefit one of the highest *minimum* old-age incomes in the industrial world. Including the "tax offset" for seniors that fully shelters the Age Pension, the program replaces nearly 45 percent of the median worker's after-tax earnings. The expanded Australian Age Pension, Whiteford and Stanton (2002) observe, "is actually closer to a demogrant, with a progressive income-test to exclude the relatively well-off." What was once a welfare grant to the poor became a benefit claimed by the great majority, as a matter of right, in return for a lifetime's contribution to the nation (Bateman and Piggott 2001a; Commonwealth Treasury of Australia 2001, 2002; King et al. 1999; Rein and Turner 2001; Whiteford and Stanton 2002).

The expansion of Age Pension benefits also acted as a powerful incentive to retire. For earnings within the taper, a worker was effectively taxed 40 percent—via the loss of Age Pension benefits—before accounting for income taxes and the direct and indirect costs of working.[1] Because of the falling demand for older workers and the expansion of the Age Pension program, earnings only accounted for 3 percent of old-age income in 1986, versus 16 percent 15 years earlier (Table 5.1) (King et al. 1999; OECD Labour Market Statistics 2003).

While the expanded Age Pension provided a relatively generous minimum old-age income, it was designed as a means-tested safety net, not a program to replace preretirement earnings. Many Australians thus faced a significant decline in living standards over the increasingly lengthy period of retirement. The nation's welfare approach to old-age incomes had clearly reached its limit (Commonwealth Treasury of Australia 2001; King et al. 1999).

To provide more adequate retirement incomes, a government commission in 1976 proposed the creation of an earnings-related social insurance program, but the proposal gained little support. Many liberals opposed the plan because lower-income workers would be forced to contribute but get little or no additional income above the Age Pension benefit. Moreover, oil shocks and overseas competition produced large deficits in the nation's trade balance and the government budget. Reducing the twin deficits required cuts in public expenditures and increased private saving. It was therefore not the time to create a large public pension program, financed on a pay-as-you-go basis, that could undermine private saving.

The government indeed scaled back the Age Pension program. It tightened the means test to reduce or eliminate allowances for better-off retirees. It also froze the "free area" in nominal dollars, even though inflation at the time was running over 10 percent. The basic structure of the Age Pension program has changed little since these reforms in the mid-1980s and is presented in Box 5.1 (Bateman and Piggot 1997, 2001a; Commonwealth Treasury of Australia 2001; Whiteford and Stanton 2002).

Table 5.1 Sources of Retirement Income, Australian Households Age 65 or Older, 1969, 1986, and 1996 (%)

Source	1969	1986	1996
Government cash benefits	65	79	77
Earnings	16	3	3
Capital income	19	18	20

SOURCE: King et al. (1999), using Australian Bureau of Statistics Income Survey data.

Box 5.1 Australian Age Pension Benefits, 2005

Benefits to each person
Single   A$12,711 per year
Married   A$10,613 per year

Benefits indexed to greater of the Consumer Price Index or male
average earnings.

Income or asset test (whichever results in a lower benefit)
Income test
Pension withdrawn at the rate of 40 cents for each A$1 of private
income in excess of a free area of:

Single   A$62 per week (A$3,224 per year)
Married   A$110 per week (A$5,720 per year)

Asset test
Pension withdrawn by A$1.50 per week for every A$1,000 of
financial assets above the following thresholds:

	Homeowner	Nonhomeowner
Single	A$157,000	A$270,500
Married	A$223,000	A$336,500

Income and asset thresholds and limits indexed to prices.

Australian incomes denominated in Australian dollars are comparable to U.S. incomes denominated in U.S. dollars. Between
2001 and 2005, the exchange rate has fluctuated between A$2
and A$1.2 to US$1.

SOURCE: Centrelink (2005).

THE REFORM OF THE AUSTRALIAN RETIREMENT INCOME SYSTEM: EVOLUTION OF INDIVIDUAL ACCOUNTS

While the debate over public old-age benefits proceeded, the Australian labor movement stepped up demands for expanded coverage under employer-based plans. By the early 1980s, this campaign helped lift overall pension coverage to 42 percent of the workforce. The largest gains came in multi-employer "industry plans" in which the union had a strong if not dominant voice (Bateman and Piggot 1997; Commonwealth Treasury of Australia 2001; Whiteford and Stanton 2002).

When a Labor government returned to power in 1983, it adopted the tack of using employer plans to address the nation's old-age income problem. Its key leverage point was the annual negotiation over the national standard labor contract between the representatives of labor and management. Australia, like many nations on the European continent, had such national bargaining. In the 1986 negotiations, the government collaborated with the unions to win a 3 percent "award superannuation" pension contribution in lieu of a comparable increase in wages.[2] After the High Court ruled in 1989 that pensions could indeed be included in the wage-setting process, award superannuation contributions were widely adopted in renegotiated labor agreements. Participation in employer plans, as a result, reached 72 percent of wage and salary workers by the end of the 1980s.

In Europe, such negotiations had resulted in mandatory pension institutions in which contributions were required as a matter of law. In Australia, however, the national labor agreement did not carry the same weight. Rather, it served as a model that was generally adopted in bargaining conducted at the firm or industry level. Because the pension contribution in the model contract was a direct substitute for wages and a uniform percent of earnings across industries and firms, the plans to emerge were overwhelmingly individual account defined-contribution arrangements. Because they grew out of labor negotiations, the funds tended to be invested collectively in employer or industrywide funds and employees participated in the management of those funds (Bateman and Piggot 2001b; Commonwealth Treasury of Australia 2001).

While promoting employer plans, the government also reformed the general "framework for retirement income policy" (Commonwealth

Treasury of Australia 2001). It imposed ERISA-like rules, such as full and immediate vesting of award superannuation contributions, equal labor-management representation on the boards overseeing the new superannuation award "industry" funds, and a "prudent man" investment management standard (Commonwealth Treasury of Australia 2001).

The government also reformed Australia's system of retirement plan taxation. As in many other countries, employer contributions to retirement plans were tax deductible, investment income was tax exempt, and benefits taxed to the beneficiary upon receipt. But, if workers in Australia took their benefit as a lump sum at retirement, only five percent of the total amount was subject to tax. With the expansion of the funded employer plans, this involved a significant loss of government revenues.

Lump-sum payouts also allowed beneficiaries to use or invest these funds in ways that maximized access to Age Pension benefits. This practice, known as "double dipping," had become more attractive with the expanded availability of Age Pension benefits and the growth of employer plan coverage. Given this favorable tax treatment and double dipping opportunities, the great majority of Australians covered by employer plans have taken their benefit as a lump sum (Commonwealth Treasury of Australia 2001).

To reduce the size of rapidly expanding pension tax expenditures, the government imposed a 15 percent tax on contributions, investment income, and payouts from employer plans. Distributions received before age 55—the designated "preservation age"—were assessed an additional 15 percent tax, as were contributions made by individuals earning more than designated amounts and distributions exceeding designated amounts (approximately A$124,720 in 2004/2005) (Commonwealth Treasury of Australia 2001).

To combat double dipping, the government introduced "deeming" in the Age Pension means test. Deeming imputed income to assets that generated little or no cash income, such as checking accounts and nondividend paying stock. As the Age Pension income test had been more stringent than its asset test, deeming created a more consistent and meaningful evaluation of means (Commonwealth Treasury of Australia 2001).

The final step in the development of the new Australian system was to ramp up the program. When the award superannuation program was introduced in 1986, it was understood that the 3 percent contribution was the first installment of a program to set aside 9 percent or more in an individual retirement account. A 3 percent contribution could not generate very much retirement income. The overhead costs involved in handling such small sums were also quite onerous, so the government and the unions proposed a 6 percent contribution in the 1989 national wage-setting negotiations. The agency overseeing the negotiating process balked, however, citing spotty compliance with the existing 3 percent contribution program (Bateman and Piggot 2001a).

The government, at this point, decided to abandon the collective bargaining approach. In 1991, it enacted the Superannuation Guarantee mandatory individual account program, to be put in place the following year. The government now required employers to make a pension contribution, with the minimum contribution rising to 9 percent of covered earnings by 2002, on earnings between A$5,400 and A$80,000, indexed to wage growth.[3] The resulting funds would typically be invested collectively, in a company or industry fund overseen by employer and employee trustees. The Labor government in 1995 proposed an increase in the ultimate contribution to 15 percent of earnings, adding an additional 3 percent from employees, matched by an additional 3 percent from the government. The return of the Conservatives in 1996 ended this initiative (Whiteford and Stanton 2002).

This Superannuation Guarantee program—the direct extension of the negotiated award superannuation program of the 1980s—is now viewed as the core of Australia's retirement income system. The means-tested Age Pension and voluntary employer plans remain critically important to lower and higher paid workers, respectively. But the Superannuation Guarantee program, and the regulatory framework developed over the past 20 years, is widely viewed as the centerpiece of the Australian retirement income system.

AN ASSESSMENT OF THE REFORMED AUSTRALIAN SYSTEM

The reform of the Australian retirement income system, centered on the introduction of the Superannuation Guarantee program, had three main objectives: 1) to provide more adequate old-age incomes, 2) to re-strain public expenditures on the elderly, and 3) to improve the system's alignment with the labor market.

The Superannuation Guarantee program will clearly create a significant retirement asset and more adequate old-age incomes. As the program matures, capital market investments will become a key source of income for the entire elderly population. The program will diversify their retirement income portfolios and reduce their exposure to political risk that a large social insurance program entails—that is, the possibility that an overburdened future government would cut promised benefits. In addition, workers will have access to the Age Pension and continuing employer programs.

The Australian Treasury has projected the retirement income provided by the Superannuation Guarantee program when the program matures, i.e., when workers have contributed over their entire careers. For the hypothetical median worker, contributing 9 percent over a 40-year career will produce a nominal (non-inflation-proofed) annuity at age 65 equal to about 90 percent of the full Age Pension benefit. (Workers are not required to annuitize their Superannuation Guarantee balances in this fashion, but the assumption greatly simplifies the analysis.) Such an annuity would produce an estimated 30 percent loss of Age Pension benefits due to the means test at the time of retirement. The worker's combined retirement income would then replace 53 percent of pretax and 66 percent of final after-tax earnings (Table 5.2).

The Treasury also explored retirement income over a projected 18 years of retirement. During this period, the Age Pension is indexed to wage growth, so its real (after-inflation) value rises over time. Meanwhile, the real value of the nominal superannuation guarantee annuity steadily declines. The median worker would thus see a steady rise in means-tested Age Pension benefits. Over the full 18 years of retirement, this worker is projected to collect 92 percent of full Age Pension benefits, with the two programs together replacing 83 percent of final after-tax earnings. The effect of the Superannuation Guarantee program should thus be a substantial increase in retirement incomes, with the major contribution coming in the early years of retirement and declining over time.[4]

These Treasury projections are point estimates and carry a great deal of uncertainty. Workers clearly bear significant financial risks in

Table 5.2   Retirement Income for Hypothetical Median Worker in the New Australian System

Retirement income	Percent of	
	Age Pension benefit	Preretirement earnings
At age 65		
Superannuation Guarantee annuity income	90	
Age Pension benefit	70	
Combined retirement income	160	
Pretax replacement rate		53
After-tax replacement rate		66
Across remaining expected lifetime		
Age Pension benefit	92	
Combined after-tax replacement rate		83
Assumptions[a]		
Full Age Pension is equal to 1/3 median earnings		
Real rate of return on assets	4.5	
Real rate of wage growth	1.5	
Rate of inflation	2.5	

NOTE: This projection is for a worker with median earnings (75 percent of male total average weekly earnings) who contributes 9 percent of earnings to a Superannuation Guarantee account over a 40-year career and retires at age 65.
[a] Superannuation Guarantee annuity income is calculated as an actuarially fair nominal annuity using 75 percent of the worker's account balance at retirement, at age 65.
SOURCE: Commonwealth Treasury of Australia (2002).

the individual account program. Even if the Treasury's point estimates prove accurate on average, outcomes will vary both within and between generational cohorts. Collective investment and the control of investment policy by pension fund trustees subject to the "prudent man" investment standard reduce this risk for most Superannuation Guarantee participants. But a trend toward greater employee choice and smaller funds should increase the dispersion of individual results. Workers are also exposed to the risk that their cohort will experience unusually poor investment returns (Bateman and Piggot 1997).

The means-tested Age Pension provides a measure of protection against these risks. Unlucky individuals or cohorts get higher means-tested benefits, with the cost borne by all active workers (in the form of higher taxes) and by elderly individuals and cohorts who had better luck in their investments (through lower Age Pension benefits). As in any insurance program, the availability of this protection creates a moral hazard. Participants could be induced to take on more risk than they otherwise might, as they get to keep relatively more of any gain and less of any loss. For example, low earners, on the cusp between a full Age Pension and the 40 percent taper, keep 60 percent of any gain but bear none of any loss. Similarly, high earners, on the cusp between the 40 percent taper and an income too high to qualify for Age Pension benefits, get the entire gain but absorb only 60 percent of any loss. The most serious financial risk in the Australian system could be in the decumulation process because the Superannuation Guarantee program does not require that balances be annuitized. Without annuitization, the elderly face the risk of consuming their assets too quickly or of consuming too little to the point of hardship. The government has tried to induce annuitization using tax incentives and the rules of the Age Pension means test, but the response thus far has been disappointing. Various experts thus expect that Australia, at some point, will mandate the annuitization of at least a portion of Superannuation Guarantee account balances. Such a policy would make annuities more affordable, by reducing adverse selection and marketing costs. It would also assure that the Superannuation Guarantee program, mandated by the government and supported by tax benefits, fulfills its intended purpose of converting income from earnings into a secure income in retirement.[5]

A second objective of the Australian reform was to restrain the growth of public expenditures on the elderly. Australia currently allocates a fairly low 3 percent of GDP to its public Age Pension program. The Treasury projects this expense to rise to 4.7 percent of GDP by 2050 as the population ages. Without the Superannuation Guarantee program, however, projected Age Pension expenditures would reach 6.8 percent of GDP. Because of the income generated by the Superannuation Guarantee program, the Treasury projects that 1) the share of the elderly receiving no Age Pension benefit will rise from 18 percent today to about 25 percent in 2050, 2) the share getting a partial benefit will rise from a quarter to about 40 percent, and 3) the share collecting a full Age Pension benefit will fall from over half to about a third (Commonwealth Treasury of Australia 2002; Mitchell and O'Quinn 1997).

Offsetting these savings in government expenditures is the cost of subsidizing the Superannuation Guarantee program through generous tax favors. While the tax changes of the 1980s significantly reduced the government's revenue loss, the Treasury's projections show tax expenditures on the Superannuation Guarantee program exceeding reductions in Age Pension expenditures through 2020, after which the balance becomes increasingly favorable (Commonwealth Treasury of Australia 2002).

A third objective of the Australian reform was to improve the system's alignment with the labor market. A major drawback of the Age Pension is the powerful retirement incentive the program creates. A worker cannot increase future benefits by delaying retirement past age 65, and any earnings above a minimal amount will then result in a significant benefit reduction.

Potentially more troublesome is the incentive the Age Pension creates to retire early, as most Australians already retire well before age 65. The program gives workers a higher Age Pension benefit if they retire early, live off their savings, and thus reduce the effect of the means test administered at age 65. If workers respond to this incentive, it would reduce the resources of the retirement income system while increasing its burdens. Workers who are out of the labor force do not pay taxes that fund the Age Pension, nor do they contribute to their Superannuation Guarantee accounts, and lowering the balances in those accounts reduces the investment income they earn. Additional time spent out of the labor force also stretches the period of "retirement" those accounts must support. Because workers arrive at age 65 with smaller balances, the government is required to make up a portion of the deficiency through increased Age Pension benefits.

Australian men currently withdraw from career employment at age 58, significantly earlier than the age assumed in the Treasury model. Most experts cite the declining demand for older men, as seen throughout the industrial world, and the availability of special government unemployment and disability benefits for older workers. But Australia's powerful "double dipping" tradition, where workers take retirement benefits as a lump sum and deploy the proceeds in ways designed to increase Age Pension benefits, also clearly plays a role (Australian Bureau of Statistics 2004; Edey and Simon 1996).

The government is trying to counter this early-retirement incentive but with limited success. It is phasing in a rise in the Superannuation Guarantee "preservation age"—the earliest age a worker can draw down their balances without penalty—from 55 to 60. However, the higher preservation age will not be fully phased in until 2025. Its impact should also be small because the bulk of the time spent in early retirement comes between the ages of 60 and 65.[6] Moreover, Australians have long viewed retirement plan balances in lump-sum terms and have fought to maintain access to these funds. They have also come to see Age Pension benefits as a broad-based entitlement—as compensation for contributing to the nation during their working careers—and are quite comfortable arranging their affairs to maximize Age Pension benefits. Neutralizing the incentive created by the Age Pension/Superannuation Guarantee interaction thus remains a serious challenge.

CONCLUSION

The Australian example clearly illustrates the importance of size. The Australian and emerging British retirement income systems are both based on means-tested public benefits and mandated contributions to individual accounts, but Australia's system is bigger. It provides higher minimum public pensions, and it mandates larger contributions to private retirement accounts. Not surprisingly, it is projected to produce significantly more retirement income than the smaller British system.

This difference in size results in a significant difference in the perception of the public means-tested program. Australia's ample Age Pension is widely seen as a universal demogrant—a standard payment made to all elderly residents—with a tax-like clawback for the better-off portion of the population. Britain's means-tested pension credit, on the other hand, is a clear extension of the nation's welfare program—with the base payment a welfare-level allowance and much more stigma attached to benefit receipt. By midcentury, about three-fourths of the elderly in both nations is projected to be on means-tested benefits at any point in time, and a greater share at some point in their lives. Because benefits in Britain will remain at welfare levels, this stigma is unlikely to dissipate.

Despite the greater generosity of Australia's public pension program, government expenditures are projected to run about the same as in Britain and the United States, at about 5 percent of GDP. In part this is because Australia's public program is more thoroughly means tested. Only a bit more than half of the elderly in Australia currently get a full Age Pension benefit and nearly 20 percent get no public pension at all. In Britain, all workers get the Basic State Pension, no matter how affluent. Public pensions in the United Kingdom will become more targeted going forward as the Basic State Pension declines and the pension credit expands, but public pensions in Australia will also become more targeted as the Superannuation Guarantee program matures. Only a third of the elderly is then projected to get a full Age Pension, and a quarter is projected to get no public pension at all.[7]

A striking feature of the Australian reform has been the government's ability to extract a substantial portion of earnings for retirement saving—the 9 percent Superannuation Guarantee contribution—with relatively little resistance. A key contributing factor was the lack of a national social insurance program with a substantial payroll tax. The Superannuation Guarantee program also extended or replaced preexisting employer programs that covered a significant majority of Australian workers—far more than the share of workers covered by U.S. employer plans. The Superannuation Guarantee program was also comparatively cheap to administer. It had significantly lower overhead costs than British personal pensions because its larger contributions were mainly collected and managed through employers, rather than through policies marketed to individual workers. Costs were also lower than U.S. 401(k) plans because the program is mandatory, which allowed for greater economies of scale and lowered marketing costs.[8] Australia's introduction of the new mandatory retirement savings program was also eased by the sense of ownership and equity created by individual accounts and by the run-up in the stock market in the boom years of the 1990s.

Many Australians had hoped that the Superannuation Guarantee program would dominate the nation's retirement income system—that workers would accumulate enough wealth in their retirement accounts to return the Age Pension to its original safety-net function. This might have been plausible had the program expanded beyond a 9 percent contribution. But, under the current set-up, the Treasury projections have only 25 percent of the elderly collecting no Age Pension benefits at any point in time, and even fewer collecting no Age Pension at any point in their lives. The income from Superannuation Guarantee accounts also carries a good deal of risk. So, even after the program matures, the Age Pension will remain critically important both as the primary source of old-age income and as insurance against adverse financial shocks.

The major weaknesses in the Australian system—the complications arising from the interaction between the Age Pension and Superannuation Guarantee programs at the work/retirement divide—are also related to size. Australia combines means testing and individual accounts in a system large enough to maintain a reasonable approximation of preretirement living standards. The sums are of such significance that a large and rapidly growing industry has emerged to help workers invest their lump sum distributions in ways that reduce taxation and increase Age Pension benefits. This distorts the allocation of capital—typically toward housing, consumer durables, and financial products that are designed to reduce taxes and increase Age Pension benefits, and away from stocks and bonds issued by the business sector. The outlays for financial planning and the misallocation of capital are significant additional costs in the operation of Australia's retirement income system.

The Australian system also creates a powerful incentive to retire early. The Age Pension, designed as a welfare program, uses a means test to identify the needy and provide a basic old-age allowance. Such means-tested programs generate a moral hazard. They discourage work and saving because the income that work and saving produces reduces the means-tested benefit. So long as the benefit and withdrawal threshold is low, as in standard welfare programs, the bulk of the population might be expected to ignore the moral hazard. After Australia expanded the Age Pension and introduced the taper, however, the bulk of the population clearly altered its behavior to increase their means-tested benefits. As the Superannuation Guarantee program matures and balances mount, so will the incentive to retire early, live off accumulated assets, and claim a larger government pension. This early retirement response will undermine the effectiveness of the Age Pension means test, and unnecessarily increase government expenditures, while significantly reducing retirement incomes.

Notes

1. The "free area" in the 1970s was roughly equal to the full Age Pension benefit. As the free area threshold was indexed to prices and the Age Pension to wages, the free area has since fallen to about 25 percent of the Age Pension benefit (Whiteford and Bond 1999).
2. Substituting pension contributions for increased cash wages increased saving, which helped lower inflation, interest rates, and the nation's widening trade deficit.
3. Accruals in funded defined-benefit plans are a permissible substitute, but they require an "actuarial benefit certificate" indicating that participants receive equal or greater value than they would under the Superannuation Guarantee program.
4. For workers earning 100 percent of "male total average weekly earnings," the two programs together would initially replace an estimated 54 percent of final after-tax earnings and an estimated 73 percent of final after-tax earnings over the 18 years of retirement (Commonwealth Treasury of Australia 2002).
5. If Australia mandated annuitization, it would have to decide whether to mandate gender-neutral annuity rates. Women tend to have lower lifetime earnings and therefore lower Superannuation Guarantee accumulations. They also have greater expected longevity. Gender-specific annuity rates would thus result in retirement incomes that were far lower for women than for men. One Australian observer noted that low-wage workers also have low expected longevity. Mandatory annuitization that fails to take this into account would, in effect, transfer income from the poor to the rich (Bateman and Piggott 2001a; King et al. 1999).
6. The primary sources of "early retirement" income have been generous disability and unemployment benefits. The disability benefits are asset tested, so the build-up of significant Superannuation Guarantee assets, available at age 60, would reduce moral hazard in the disability program and discourage its use as a pathway out of the labor force. Means-testing "mature age" unemployed benefits would have a similar effect. Raising the Superannuation Guarantee preservation age to 65, thus eliminating the gap with the Age Pension program, would exclude Superannuation Guarantee assets from the disability and a "mature age" benefits means tests. Requiring the annuitization of Superannuation Guarantee balances would reduce this early retirement incentive. By creating an income stream more readily subjected to the Age Pension means test, it reduces the opportunity to game the system by retiring early and running down Superannuation Guarantee assets. Applying the means test to the annuity value of the assets, not their deemed investment income, would do the same (Bateman and Piggot 1997).
7. The current cost of Australia's public pension program (3 percent of GDP) is also below expenditures in Britain because of its relatively young population. It is below expenditures in the United States primarily because of means testing.
8. Overhead costs remain an issue, nevertheless, for low-wage workers and small employers.

6
Lessons from Canada

Investing the Trust Fund in Equities

Canada introduced equity investments into its Social Security program by using the "trust fund investment" approach; it was the first of the four Anglo-Saxon nations under review to expand its retirement income system. The legislation was enacted by the end of the 1960s. Canada's response to demographic transition, however, came late, in 1997. In that year, Canada restored solvency to its social insurance program by accelerating scheduled tax increases to prefund future benefits and by investing some of the accumulated assets in equities.

To achieve a specified retirement income objective, using the social insurance trust fund as a vehicle for investing equities has significant financial advantages over the use of individual accounts. This approach, however, raises serious political issues, given the power it potentially puts in the hands of government. Canada adopted an elaborate governance design, taken largely from the governance of employer defined-benefit plans, to minimize political involvement in the management of trust fund assets. Although the system has been in place for only a few years, the Canadian experience to date suggests that the problem is manageable. It also appears considerably less daunting than governing equity investments in a myriad of Social Security individual accounts.

CANADIAN SYSTEM AT THE END OF THE 1980s

For the first two decades of the postwar period, Canada had a simple Anglo-Saxon two-tier retirement income system. The first tier was the public Old Age Security program, which had evolved out of Canada's 1927 means-tested welfare program for the elderly. Old Age Security was not a social insurance program, funded by a payroll tax, but a demogrant funded out of general revenues. The program gave all long-

term residents, age 70 and over, a basic income equal to about 15 percent of national average earnings. This amount was less than the 20
percent of national average earnings typically guaranteed by the 1927
means-tested program. But the Canadian provinces had contributed to
the older means-tested program, while Old Age Security was entirely
funded by the federal government, and most provinces supplemented
the new federal demogrant.

As in other Anglo-Saxon nations, tax-advantaged employer plans
made up the second tier in the Canadian system. Coverage grew rapidly
after the Second World War, rising from 10 to 15 percent of wage and
salary workers in the 1930s to 40 percent by 1970. The primary drivers
were much the same as in other Anglo-Saxon nations: 1) the low level
of public old-age pensions; 2) the growth of employers that traditionally offer pensions, such as governments and large corporations, and
of unions, which made pensions a high priority in postwar collective
bargaining; and 3) the expansion of income taxation, which made the
favorable treatment accorded pension saving increasingly attractive.[1]

Like other Anglo-Saxon nations, Canada also found its retirement
income system increasingly deficient toward the end of the long postwar boom. While the incomes of working-age adults rose steadily, the
elderly were left behind. They had little or no income from work or
savings, and few qualified for a reasonable employer pension. By the
early 1960s, nearly 45 percent of the elderly were classified as poor,
and the income gap between workers and their parents was widening
(Osberg 2001).

The expansion of the Canadian retirement income system in the late
1960s focused primarily on the problem of old-age poverty. Between
1965 and 1969, Canada

- Reduced the age of eligibility for Old Age Security from 70 to 65.

- Introduced a new earnings-related social insurance program, the
  Canada/Quebec Pension Plan (C/QPP). The program was funded
  by a payroll tax and, at age 65, provided a pension that replaced
  25 percent of earnings up to the national average.[2]

- Introduced an income-tested Guaranteed Income Supplement,
  which was expected to become irrelevant with the maturation of
  the C/QPP.[3]

• Broadened access and improved the security of employer pension benefits by imposing vesting, funding, and fiduciary requirements.

Further details are provided in Box 6.1.

The expanded Canadian system was quite similar to that developed in the United States. The Old Age Security and C/QPP programs combined provided the hypothetical "average earner" 40 percent of preretirement earnings, close to the 42 percent policy model replacement rate for the "average earner" in the expanded Social Security program.

The Canadian system differed from that in the United States in the unusually strong role of the provinces in pension policy and in the Canadian focus on poverty reduction. The role of the provinces is clearly seen in the regulation of employer plans and in the design of the public earnings-related pension program. The Pension Benefits Acts, which regulated employer plans, required the enactment of legislation at the provincial as well as national level. As a result, the new vesting, funding, and fiduciary requirements varied somewhat from province to province.[4] In the new public earnings-related pension program, the provinces were the designated "stewards" of the program, along with the national government. Any major reform required the approval of two-thirds of the provinces with two-thirds of the population. Because of the strength of French-Canadian nationalism in Quebec, the province was allowed to set up a separate Quebec Pension Plan (QPP), distinct from the Canada Pension Plan (CPP), so long as it had comparable benefits and contribution rates.

The expansion of the Canadian system was also highly targeted to poverty reduction. Thus C/QPP does not replace earnings above the national average. The Guaranteed Income Supplement also set a retirement income floor significantly higher than that in the United States or the United Kingdom and similar to that provided by the Australian Age Pension. Individuals who did not qualify for a full earnings-related benefit—primarily older cohorts, low-wage workers, and widows—were assured an income equal to about a third of the national average wage; couples were assured about half the national average wage. As this guaranteed income was not much below the combined benefit from the Old Age Security program and the C/QPP (Figure 6.1), the Canadian public system, as John Myles put it, "functioned approximately like a

Box 6.1   The Canadian Retirement Income System at the End of the 1970s

1) Public programs

Old Age Security:
- A flat payment of about 15 percent of average earnings provided to all long-term residents.
- Funded out of general revenues.

Canada/Quebec Pension Plan:
- A pension of 25 percent of indexed earnings, on earnings up to national average earnings.
- Funded by payroll tax of 3.6 percent on earnings between 10 and 100 percent of average earnings.

Guaranteed Income Supplement:
- An income-tested benefit that guarantees individuals age 65 and older an income equal to about a third of national average earnings, reduced by $C0.50 for each $C1 of other income.
- Funded out of general revenues.

2) Employer plans

Covered about 45 percent of wage and salary workers:
- About 31 percent of private sector wage and salary workers.
- 100 percent of public sector wage and salary workers.
- 90 percent covered by a defined-benefit plan.

Key features of Canadian employer defined-benefit plans:
- The common benefit was 2 percent of final salary per year of service, reduced by a portion of the worker's public pension.
- Mandatory vesting, typically at age 45 with 15 years of service.
- More than half required employee contributions.
- Employers topped up the funding to meet the cost of currently accrued benefits and to pay down funding deficits.

SOURCE: Coward (1995).

Figure 6.1 Canadian Government Retirement Benefits, by Quintiles, 1980

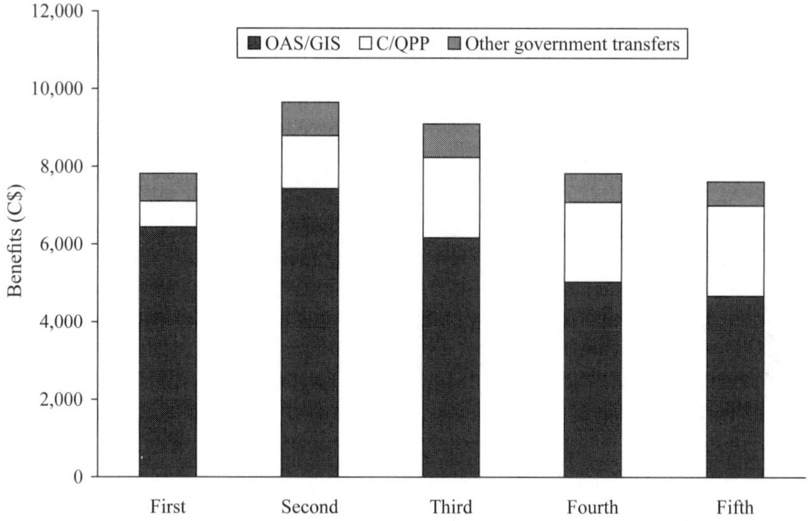

NOTE: OAS/GIS = Old Age Security/Guaranteed Income Supplement; C/QPP = Can-
ada/Quebec Pension Plan.
SOURCE: Myles (2000).

universal flat benefit system" (Battle 2003; Béland and Myles 2005;
Myles 2000, p. 14; Osberg 2001).

The Canadian public system succeeded in its objective of reducing old-age poverty. As the C/QPP program matured and delivered full
benefits to an increasing share of the elderly population, the elderly
poverty rate fell from 44 percent in 1961 to 18 percent in 1999 (Figure
6.2). However, the maturation of the C/QPP did not eliminate the need
for the Guaranteed Income Supplement, as originally envisaged. About
a third of the elderly in 2001 still received these benefits, down from
about half in 1985. These benefits are particularly important to older
widows, who continue to have incomes somewhat below, though not
far below, the official Canadian poverty line.[5]

Figure 6.2 Percent of the Elderly Population below the Canadian Poverty Line, 1961–1999

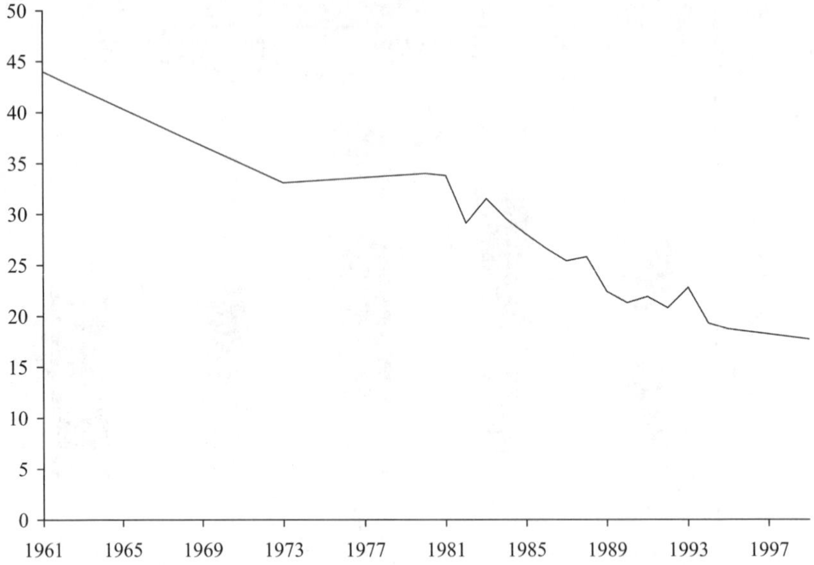

SOURCE: Osberg (2001); Ross, Scott, and Smith (2000).

THE REFORMED CANADIAN RETIREMENT SYSTEM

Canada, like other industrial nations, reformed its retirement in-come system at the end of the twentieth century in response to the greater instability in employer plans and the impending transition to a much older society. Like the United States and the United Kingdom, Canada imposed new funding regulations on employer plans to protect accrued pension benefits in the event the sponsor went bankrupt. It re-sponded to the demographic transition by reducing benefits and raising taxes. Canada's primary response to the challenge of population aging, however, was to prefund the C/QPP and invest the accumulated assets in equities.

The Reform of Employer-Sponsored Plans

Similar to other Anglo-Saxon nations, Canada imposed new regulations on employer plans to protect worker benefits should the sponsor go bankrupt. If an existing plan did not have enough assets to satisfy its termination liability—the value of pensions based on current wages, discounted to the present using the interest rate on low-risk bonds—the sponsor had to eliminate the deficit within five years.

From the enactment of the new regulations in 1987 through the end of the 1990s, the reform appeared quite successful. Financial markets were unusually robust, and most plans showed comfortable surpluses when valued on either a continuing or termination basis.[6] Employer plans were so well funded that many sponsors in Canada, as in the United States and elsewhere, used the assets to fund sweetened early retirement benefits and take extended funding holidays.

But, as we have seen, the financial condition of employer defined-benefit plans is highly sensitive to shifts in financial conditions. It took only a few years for the downturn at the beginning of the new century to pull employer defined-benefit plans deeply into the red. Watson Wyatt, the pension consulting firm, estimates that plans sponsored by companies listed on the Toronto Stock exchange had a "funding ratio" of about 115 percent at year-end 2000—that is, pension fund assets were about 15 percent greater than the present value of plan liabilities. By May 2003, plan assets covered barely 80 percent of benefit obligations, similar to the experience elsewhere. The new funding rules thus became binding, requiring sponsors to extinguish termination-valuation deficits within five years (Watson Wyatt 2004).

The new rules were largely responsible for lifting the overall funding ratio above 85 percent by year-end 2003. A recovery in stock prices increased the value of pension fund assets, but this was largely offset by continuing declines in the interest rate on the low-risk bonds used to value termination liabilities. It was the stepped-up contributions, required in response to the termination valuation deficits, that strengthened the finances of employer plans and protected the pension benefits accrued by the sponsor's workers (Watson Wyatt 2004, 2005b).

A major shortcoming in this approach to maintaining solvency, however, was the perverse pension funding pattern it created over the business cycle. During upswings, employer plans were generally given a clean bill of financial health by both the ongoing and termination solvency measures, so funding requirements were low. The government had also enacted the "excess surplus" rule, similar to rules enacted elsewhere, that prevented sponsors of apparently well-funded plans from making tax-deductible pension contributions.[7] But in economic downturns, when sponsors were financially stressed, the solvency measures flashed red and the new funding rules forced a sharp spike in contributions.

The new funding rules were especially onerous now that most employer plans were mature. They had substantial asset accumulations and their financial program called for investment income to fund about two-thirds of benefit payments.[8] The financial downturn at the turn of the century thus produced losses that dwarfed the employer's annual contribution. The demand for increased contributions during economic downturns actually contributed to the bankruptcy of weakened sponsors, with Air Canada the best known example (Le Pan 2003).[9]

As in other Anglo-Saxon nations, the demand for greater contributions in the downturn of the early 2000s accelerated the shift of employers out of defined-benefit plans. The coverage of employer defined-benefit plans had not declined as dramatically in Canada, or the United Kingdom, as it had in the United States. In 2003, about 35 percent of Canadian wage and salary workers were covered by such plans. But a 2004 survey of 68 large firms, conducted by Watson Wyatt and the Conference Board, found that nearly 40 percent of these employers had either eliminated a defined-benefit plan, converted one to a defined-contribution format, or were planning to do so (Watson Wyatt 2005b).

Of the companies in the 2004 Watson Wyatt survey with underfunded plans, nearly 60 percent had taken a contribution holiday within the past four years. Many had been prevented from contributing by the excess surplus rule, but the great majority had been happy not to contribute—implicitly accepting the solvency measurements taken at the height of the boom as the best indication of the long-term health of their plans (Watson Wyatt 2004, 2005b).

The problem with both statutory measures of solvency—both the ongoing and termination measures—is that they consider only the current value of plan assets and liabilities. They ignore the substantial risks involved in funding long-term fixed obligations with equities. As experience makes clear, the value of assets and liabilities in such plans can rapidly change in ways that dramatically reduce their ability to satisfy benefit obligations.

The Reform of the Public Pension System

Canada, like other industrial nations, responded to the impending demographic transition by reducing public old-age pension benefits and raising contributions. But because the Canadian program focused on poverty reduction, the cuts were small.[10] Canada's primary response to the challenge of population aging was the 1997 decision to prefund the C/QPP and invest the accumulated assets in equities. The reform was sparked by the government actuary's 1995 report on the program, which projected a sharp rise in benefit payments in the coming century. To fund these benefits on a pay-as-you-go basis, contributions would need to rise from the current 5.6 percent of covered earnings to 14.2 percent by 2030 (Federal, Provincial, and Territorial Governments of Canada 1996a,b).

There was significant opposition to cutting CPP benefits, primarily from the Liberal end of the political spectrum. Benefit cuts would lower Canada's retirement income floor and expand the size of the income-tested Guaranteed Income Supplement program.[11] As major reforms to the C/QPP program required the approval of two-thirds of Canada's provinces with two-thirds of the population, significant cuts were pushed off the table.

There was also stiff resistance to the nearly threefold increase in contributions required to fund benefits in 2030 on a pay-as-you-go basis. No politician wants to enact such a substantial tax increase, especially to maintain rather than increase government benefits. But the primary objection to such a tax increase, and to continued pay-as-you-go funding, was intergenerational fairness. As expressed in an overview of the problem prepared by the Federal, Provincial, and Territorial Governments of Canada, the fair approach to pension funding would have each generation contributing much the same share of earnings and in retirement getting much the same replacement rate (Federal, Provincial, and Territorial Governments of Canada 1996a,b; Pesando 2001).

The key reform of the C/QPP program enacted in 1997 thus involved a rapid rise in contributions to its projected uniform long-term rate. The rapid rise was designed to build-up the C/QPP trust fund in the near term, with income on trust fund assets augmenting contributions to pay benefits in the out-years. To increase trust fund income and reduce the long-term contribution rate, the C/QPP would invest trust fund assets in equities.[12]

The CPP funding model developed by the government actuary projects contributions, set at 9.9 percent of covered earnings, to exceed benefit payments through 2020. The aging population would then push outlays above payroll tax receipts. Contributions will cover barely 85 percent of benefit payments by the end of the 2030s, then stabilize at that level. By 2020, however, assets in the CPP trust fund should exceed five times annual outlays. With an estimated real return of 4.1 percent, CPP investment income should exceed 20 percent of annual outlays. Total inflows—tax receipts plus investment income—in fact continuously exceed outflows by a significant margin. Trust fund assets continue to rise and at the end of the planning horizon, in 2075, are projected at seven times annual benefit outlays (Office of the Chief Actuary 2004).

The decision to invest C/QPP assets in equities, with their greater expected return but also greater risk, was strongly influenced by the contrasting experience of the QPP and CPP trust funds. Both plans had accumulated assets, equal to about two years of benefit payments, as a buffer against cash flow shortfalls. Each plan also pursued a policy of "social investment"—investing trust fund assets to achieve "socially desirable" objectives in addition to traditional financial goals. And both notions of "socially desirable" reflected the influence of the Canadian provinces in national pension policy. The CPP invested its assets in non-marketable provincial bonds with a yield equal to that on federal debt. As the federal government paid a lower interest rate than the provinces, and as the bonds were not marketable, the CPP was subsidizing the provincial governments. Quebec adopted a more active social investment policy, with the QPP directed to buy equities and fund projects thought to advance the economic development of the province. Such active "social investment" strategies also tend to produce sub-par risk-adjusted returns, but the three decades in which the C/QPP programs had been in existence had been a boom period for equities. Furthermore, the QPP over time had moved away from social investing toward a policy that emphasized standard risk-adjusted return optimization. The QPP thus clearly outperformed the CPP. With this experience in the advantages of equity investments in social insurance programs, the 1997 reformers decided to invest CPP assets in equities (Béland forthcoming [2006]; Béland and Myles 2005; CPP 1997; Mendelson 2005).[13]

The 1997 CPP reform, however, rejected social investment. It defined the sole objective of the CPP Investment Board (CPPIB) as acting in the best interests of plan participants—both active and retired—under the governing notion that each generation should contribute much the same share of earnings and get much the same benefits. That investment decisions are made solely in the best interests of plan participants is the fiduciary standard that ERISA and the Canadian Pension Benefit Acts require of employer defined-benefit plans. To pursue such a policy at the CPP, the 1997 legislation created the CPPIB Board, a quasi-independent agency explicitly modeled on the "institutional investor" governance system that ERISA and the Pension Benefits Acts mandate for publicly regulated employer plans. In addition to defining participants as the sole beneficiaries of the plan, this governance system requires the CPPIB to "exercise the care, diligence and skill that a reasonably prudent person would exercise in comparable circumstances" when handling plan assets and to provide periodic performance reports to assure accountability (CPPIB 1997; Slater 1997b).

The 1997 legislation defined an elaborate set of procedures designed to make the CPPIB as independent from the government as possible. To name the members of the investment board, the participating provincial governments, as "stewards" of the program, would each select one member of the nominating committee. That committee would draw up a list of candidates that excluded government officials and included investment professionals. The federal Minister of Finance, in consultation with the provincial Ministers of Finance, would then select the investment board members. To assure efficiency, transparency, and public accountability, the board was required to conduct periodic internal performance reviews, issue quarterly and annual financial reports, organize biennial town meetings in each province, and undergo a thorough triennial review (CPP 1997; Slater 1997b).

The CPPIB has embraced the institutional investor model. "As a long-term investor, with substantial annual cash inflows for the next twenty years," it intends to "build a broad-based portfolio" that includes not just investments in stocks and bonds, but also in merchant banking, real estate, infrastructure projects, venture capital, private equity, and buyout funds (CPPIB 2003). The investment board also intends to become active in corporate governance under the notion that "the thoughtful voting of our proxies can constructively influence corporate performance and have a positive impact on the value of our portfolio" (CPPIB 2005).

AN ASSESSMENT OF THE REFORMED CANADIAN SYSTEM

It is too early to evaluate the success of the 1997 reform to the CPP program and its new funding model. The primary concerns, however, are in managing the financial and political risks inherent in a social insurance program funded with equities.

In terms of managing the financial risks, one thing is clear. The CPP and other social insurance programs should be managed quite differently than employer defined-benefit plans. This is clearly indicated in the way financial health is evaluated. In employer plans, the standard measure of solvency is the funded ratio. Whether evaluated on an ongoing or termination basis, the basic question is whether the assets in the pension fund are sufficient to pay promised benefits. In social insurance programs, by contrast, the basic solvency measure is whether the current level of contributions is sufficient, given the financial structure of the program, to pay promised benefits. Thus, the U.S. Social Security program in 2006 faces a shortfall over the 75-year planning horizon equal to 2 percent of covered earnings. The reason why social insurance programs are evaluated this way is because the government is presumed to continue indefinitely. Thus, the retirement income benefits earned by workers do not need to be secured against the bankruptcy of the sponsor with assets held in a segregated pension fund.

As we have seen, equity investments make the funded ratio a weak measure of solvency and expose employer defined-benefit plans to powerful risks. The introduction of equity investments exposes the CPP, like other retirement income programs, to three types of risk: 1) the standard risk that year-to-year returns will fluctuate around the expected long-run rate and could even be negative for a considerable stretch of time, 2) the risk that the long-run rate of return could be less than expected, and 3) the risk that the plan's financial managers are infected by euphoria in booms and trepidation in busts.

The CPP is actually in a very strong position for managing the first type of risk. If the required triennial review identifies a funding shortfall, similar to that caused by the financial downturn at the turn of the century, the 1997 legislation included an automatic adjustment mechanism that restores solvency by freezing benefits and raising the contribution rate. The political system could enact a different response, but the stabilizer is a guarantee that the CPP's finances will not go off the rails.[14]

The required adjustments, moreover, would not be as draconian as those required of employer plans in the early twenty-first century. As the government is presumed to continue indefinitely, the automatic stabilizer would restore balance over a 100-year period—not the five years given to employer plans with termination valuation deficits. The CPP is also far less reliant on investment income than a mature employer plan, and thus less vulnerable to the risk in investment returns. The funding model projects investment income ultimately providing over 20 percent of CPP inflows, with total inflows 10 to 15 percent greater than projected outlays. In mature employer plans, by contrast, investment income is generally more than twice as large as employer contributions. Financial fluctuations should thus have a much more moderate effect on CPP solvency.[15]

The second financial risk—that the long-run rate of return on assets is less than projected—presents a more serious problem. To protect against this risk, the CPP funding model assumes a conservative 50–50 allocation of equities and bonds and a conservative 4.1 percent real return on trust fund assets. Using these conservative assumptions, the model also projects substantial cash-flow surpluses and a rising ratio of assets to outlays. If investment returns do decline to the point where the actuarial review finds the 9.9 percent contribution rate inadequate, the automatic adjustment mechanism would restore balance by freezing benefits and raising the contribution rate (Ambachtsheer 1996; Sarney and Preneta 2001–2002; Slater 1997a). The government could also enact a different set of adjustments, for example, raising taxes or cutting benefits in a different way.

The CPP funding model also requires disciplined long-term investment management at the CPPIB, and thus far it has had such a policy.

Even though investment returns were extremely volatile over the early years of the reform (see Figure 6.3), the CPPIB has functioned as a solid long-term investor. Remarking in the 2004 Annual Report, the CPPIB stated that "A large part of the reversal in the CPP's investment fortunes . . . was the result of our decision to continue to build the equity portfolio throughout the market collapse that began in the fall of 2000 and continued to the spring of 2003, one of the worst declines in a century. Many Canadians were concerned that we were on the wrong track and should invest in bonds, or hold cash and try to time the market bottom. Our decision to stay the course and buy shares in hundreds of Canadian and foreign companies resulted in equity gains of $7.2 billion versus a $4.1 billion loss a year earlier. For us, the stock market collapse was a buying opportunity in a long investment journey."

From a purely financial perspective, the government is thus in a far better position than employers to manage the risk of equity investment

Figure 6.3 Canadian Pension Plan Investment Returns, 2000–2005

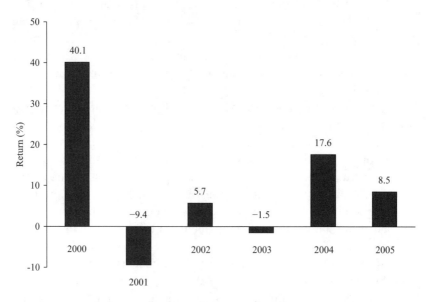

NOTE: If $C100 were invested at the beginning of 2000 and experienced these returns, its value would be $C169 at the end of 2005. This would be an internal rate of return of 8.7 percent per annum.
SOURCE: CPPIB (2005).

in a defined-benefit pension program. And, in terms of managing investment risk, the government is light years better than individuals with individual retirement accounts.

In addition to financial risks, another concern is the political risk inherent in using the trust fund as the vehicle for introducing equities into the social security program. The CPPIB was designed as an "institutional investor," no different from the investment boards of employer defined-benefit plans. Researchers have identified four ways in which government influence could turn public pension reserve managers, like the CPPIB, into something other than a standard institutional investor. The four risks are that the CPP would (Palacios 2002):

1) Become a captive source of credit that would fund the government rather than invest in assets better suited to a long-term retirement income program and would do so at below-market rates. This was clearly the case in the initial CPP funding program, which only bought Provincial government bonds and subsidized provincial borrowing. Such a policy clearly sacrificed the financial health of the pension program. To the extent that it increased government spending, it also reversed the contribution to national saving created by the funding program.

2) Invest in "socially desirable" projects and/or avoid "socially undesirable" projects. This was clearly the case in the Quebec pension, which explicitly targeted investments designed to advance the provincial and French-Canadian economy. This policy also resulted in subpar risk-adjusted returns. By introducing a diffuse new set of objectives, other than the standard financial goals, it also made it more difficult to oversee and manage the QPP.

3) Use its power as a major shareholder to promote "socially desirable" and/or avoid "socially undesirable" corporate decisions. Such decisions could involve plant closings, purchasing decisions, union recognition, lobbying practices, charitable contributions, and the like. In addition to sacrificing financial performance and diminishing the nation's ability to oversee the CPPIB, this policy could give government a tremendous lever of control over Canada's economy and society.

4) Prop up financial markets in a "crisis." In addition to sacrificing returns and weakening the governance of the CPPIB, such interventions require enormous amounts of capital and are rarely effective.

Most Canadian observers see the adoption of such policies at the CPPIB as highly unlikely. Because of the explicit "institutional investor" mandates included in the 1997 legislation, and the elaborate governance and reporting structures, the CPPIB is widely regarded as professional, independent, and accountable.

Some critics contend that the government has too little influence on the CPPIB. They worry that the "institutional investor" model unduly strengthens the hand of "capital" against competing, and weaker, "socially desirable" interests. Such critics have objected, for example, to CPP investments in Talisman Energy, a large Canadian oil and gas producer with operations in Sudan. Because Talisman funded the Sudanese government's widely criticized military campaigns, the U.S. government threatened to bar it from U.S. financial markets. Critics also object to CPP investments in buyout funds that finance corporate restructurings that result in layoffs and plant closings. Members of Parliament have also called for "ethical" screens, which would restrict investments in tobacco companies and providers of other "socially undesirable" products (Cooke 2003; Social Investment Organization 2002).

Calls for a more "socially responsible" investment policy will no doubt continue. In time, this could result in a change in the CPPIB's mandate. The acceptance of "social investment" as a policy objective might advance Canada's larger public policy objectives. Such a change, however, would clearly jeopardize the CPP funding model and its contribution to retirement income security.

CONCLUSION

The Canadian retirement income system is distinguished by 1) the relatively narrow focus of government programs on assuring a basic old-age income with minimal income-testing, 2) the long reliance on both general revenues and a payroll tax to fund these programs, and

3) its recent policy of investing social insurance trust fund assets in equities.

Canadian public pensions, even after the expansion in the late 1960s, were modest and largely targeted to low and middle earners. Even more than public pensions in the United States and the United Kingdom, Canada had little "fat" to cut when programs for the elderly came under pressure after 1980.

The Canadian system is also distinguished by its long reliance on both general revenues and a payroll tax to finance old-age pensions. This mixed revenue base gave Canada the flexibility to develop a mixed fiscal response to the demographic transition. It increased the C/QPP payroll tax and built up the program trust funds with the goal of stabilizing the long-term contribution rate. The Old Age Security and Guaranteed Income Supplement programs remain pay-as-you-go programs funded out of general revenues, so their claim on government budgets will rise as the population ages. But general revenues are drawn from a far broader base than the payroll tax. As the population ages, the government can spread the burden and raise taxes that produce the least adverse effects.

Canada's third distinguishing characteristic is its use of the social insurance trust fund to introduce equity investments into its social security program. Britain prefunded social insurance obligations with equities by encouraging employers and workers to "contract out" of SERPS (the British analog to the C/QPP), using employer plans or individual account private pensions. Australia never created an earnings-based social insurance program but mandated an individual account system to prefund, with equities, a similar earnings-related retirement income stream.

From a purely financial perspective, the Canadian trust fund approach seems best. It captures the substantial economies of scale in investment management better than employer defined-benefit plans, let alone individual worker accounts. The trust fund is in an especially good position to pool and manage the risks in equities, as it can smooth volatility over an infinite horizon. Unlike employer plans, the trust fund approach involves no additional administrative expense to maintain individual accounts or employee defined-benefit accruals. It avoids the significant marketing costs seen in employer individual account programs. Finally, it avoids the costly process of enforcing and complying with government regulations needed to distribute and secure tax-favored employee plan benefits while minimizing the revenue loss to the Treasury.

The primary objection to the trust fund approach is political. Critics in the United States generally contend that it is impossible to build up a social insurance trust fund, let alone have it invest in equities, without succumbing to one of the pitfalls cited by Palacios (2002). They claim that the U.S. Social Security trust fund has functioned as a "captive source of credit"—that the fund's build up of government bonds merely funded increased government expenditures, without raising national saving. Critics view the prospect of trust fund investment in equities with an even more jaundiced eye. The great fear is that the government would use the trust fund as an instrument for advancing public policy or the policy of the politicians who happen to be in power.

The Canadian experience provides an example of a governance structure that responds to many of these objections. The 1997 reform gave the investment board substantial independence and a clear financial objective—to minimize the long-term level contribution rate. It also provided reporting mechanisms to help maintain accountability. Most observers agree that the investment board has thus far managed trust fund assets in an independent, professional, and accountable fashion. Overseeing the management of the CPPIB has not only been far less costly than overseeing the operation of employer plans or employee individual accounts, it has also been far more effective.

Canada's ability to invest trust fund assets in equities allowed it to maintain C/QPP benefits with a level contribution rate lower than it otherwise could. This is extremely important given the rapid rise in the cost of other public programs for the elderly over the next quarter century.

The trust fund approach has also allowed Canada to prefund retirement income benefits within the traditional defined-benefit structure. Equity-funded defined benefits are far more predictable than the individual account systems used in the United Kingdom or Australia. As employers shift to defined-contribution arrangements, the predictability of public benefits provides a secure retirement income floor, helping workers plan their retirement and allowing them to take more risk in their supplemental plans. For all these reasons, the Canadian system deserves careful attention.

Notes

1. In addition to the exemption of pension contributions and investment earnings, Canada also exempted the first $1,000 in annual pension benefits. Individuals age 65 and older were also entitled to an additional "age exemption" that further sheltered pension income (Béland and Myles 2005; Coward 1995).
2. Like the U.S. Social Security program, the C/QPP program was "rushed to maturity." While introduced in 1966, workers who had consistently contributed to the program could retire on a full C/QPP pension, at age 65, from 1976 onward.
3. Unlike the UK Pension Credit, the Australian Age Pension, and Canada's 1927 Old Age Pension program, the new Guaranteed Income Supplement was income-tested rather than means-tested—only income, rather than income and assets, was considered in calculating eligibility and benefit levels.
4. The most common requirements were full vesting at age 45 with 15 years of service (subsequently tightened to full vesting after 2 years of plan participation or 5 years of service); contributions that covered the cost of currently earned benefits and the amortization of any unfunded liability; and the management of pension fund assets solely in the interest of the plan beneficiaries, without regard to the interests of the sponsor. To protect surviving spouses (essentially widows), most provinces made the joint-and-survivor annuity the default payout, with the survivor getting 60 percent of the worker's initial benefit (Coward 1995).
5. The Canadian poverty line is now significantly higher than the benchmark used in the United States. In 1994, the Canadian poverty line for a family of four in a medium-sized city was $C26,650—40 percent higher than the U.S. poverty line of $C19,024 (converted to Canadian dollars on a purchasing parity basis). Thus, the Canadian poverty rate would now be significantly lower if measured using the U.S. benchmark (Battle 2003; Fisher 1995; Myles 2000; Osberg 2001; Phipps and Curtis 2000; Sarney and Prenata 2001–2002).
6. As discussed above, both the continuing and termination valuations compare plan assets to plan liabilities, with the liabilities defined as the present value of future pension obligations. The future pension obligations in a continuing valuation are based on projected earnings when workers retire or separate from the firm and are discounted to the present using the expected return on plan assets. The future pension obligations in a termination valuation are based on current earnings and are discounted to the present using the interest rate on low-risk bonds.

   These funding rules were more critical in Canada than in the United States. In the United States, accrued pension benefits are not just backed by the assets in the pension fund, but by a legal claim on the net worth of the sponsor and, up to specified limits, by the federal PBGC. In Canada, accrued pension benefits are not backed by a claim against the sponsor. Only Ontario has a pension benefit insurance program, and the level of protection is modest (Coward 1995).
7. The Canadian excess surplus rule prevented sponsors from making contributions once the value of pension fund assets exceeded 110 percent of plan liabilities. As

elsewhere, this was designed to maintain government revenues during a period of large budget deficits,

8. In 1999, the last year for which data on 5,500 U.S. employer plans are available, single-employer defined-benefit plans paid out $91 billion in benefits and held $1.65 trillion in assets. If U.S. plans were 30 percent overfunded in 1999, as was the case in the analysis of plans sponsored by 100 very large firms conducted by the pension consultant Milliman, $1.27 trillion was the "fully funded" level of assets. If 60 percent of those assets were invested in stocks with a real rate of return of 6.5 percent (the long-term U.S. rate), and 40 percent in bonds yielding a real 2.25 percent, the long-term U.S. rate, investment income would be $61 billion, or 67 percent of benefit payments (Milliman 2005; U.S. Department of Labor 2004, Tables C5, C10).

9. Recognizing the burden placed on the firm by the 1987 funding rules, Parliament enacted the Air Canada Pension Plan Solvency Deficiency Funding Regulations in August 2004, a statute that allowed Air Canada—and Air Canada alone—to pay down its termination deficit over a 10-year period (Canadian Department of Justice 2004; Watson Wyatt 2003).

10. The benefit cuts primarily targeted the well-to-do, primarily through reductions in tax reliefs for the elderly and a limited clawback, or income-tested reduction, of Old Age Security benefits. For details see Myles (2000) and Battle (2003).

11. A cut in CPP benefits would also increase the obligations on employer plans, as most were integrated with the CPP—they essentially targeted a combined public-private benefit and reduced employer pensions by a portion of the government allowance (Coward 1995).

12. CPP benefits were also reduced by a change in the indexing formula. The benefit calculation now indexed past wages to the present, with the "present" defined as average wages over the five years prior to retirement, rather than three. As a result, benefits are now sometimes estimated at 24 rather than 25 percent of indexed earnings. The reform also reduced future outlays by tightening access to CPP disability benefits. In addition to raising the contribution rate, the 1997 reform increased revenues by freezing the "exempt amount" of earnings not subject to tax. This exempt amount, which had been pegged at earnings up to 10 percent of average earnings, was now frozen at $C3,500.

13. A proper analysis of the choice between equities and bonds in a social insurance program would not focus narrowly on the experience of the CPP and QPP from the mid-1960s through the mid-1990s, but the political process rarely makes decisions based on proper analysis. Within the investment community, which is sophisticated about such issues and tends to be suspicious about government, the recognition that the QPP had essentially abandoned social investment and was professionally managed did reduce anxiety over the use of equities in the CPP (communication from John Myles).

14. The automatic stabilizer is actually seen more as a lever forcing future governments to take some sort of action that restores solvency rather than the "proper" set of trade-offs to restore CPP solvency in all situations.

15. The government could respond to a prolonged market downturn by shifting funds from general revenues. The CPP could repay this advance, and rebuild the trust fund, when returns bounced back over the long-run expected rate.

7
Conclusions

The U.S. retirement income system faces an enormous challenge, with the transition to a much older society about to begin. The now dominant 401(k) plans have not produced the accumulations that people will need for a secure retirement, and the backbone of the retirement system—Social Security—faces a long-term shortfall. The introduction of provisions, such as automatic enrollment, to make 401(k) plans more automatic and easier may improve their performance. Efforts to restore balance to the Social Security program, however, appear stymied. Many observers, for different reasons, nevertheless suggest that investment in equities should be part of the solution.

The Social Security funding deficit is equal to 2.02 percent of taxable payrolls when measured over the traditional 75-year planning horizon and 3.70 percent when calculated from now to infinity. These magnitudes are very close to those that existed in the mid-1990s when the 1994–1996 Social Security Advisory Council attempted to fix the problem. The council was caught in a dilemma. While charged with closing the financing gap, its members resisted, for different reasons, restoring balance solely by raising taxes or cutting benefits. They all resorted to a new source of revenue—namely, the higher expected return on equity investment—to help solve the financing problem.

The council produced three separate proposals: 1) invest a portion of trust fund assets in equities; 2) "add on" individual accounts, invested in equities, that would top up the reduced benefits that could be financed by the current payroll tax; and 3) "carve-out" individual accounts invested in equities, funded by redirecting a significant portion of current payroll taxes and sharply reducing the guaranteed social insurance benefit. The council, however, failed to reach a consensus around one of these plans. No action has since been taken, and these three options remain on the table. President Bush's 2005 Social Security reform proposals are a direct descendent of the carve-out individual account proposal. Many Democrats have advocated add-on individual accounts. The nation's largest membership organization for older people, the AARP, included investing 15 percent of trust fund assets in equities as part of a package to eliminate Social Security's 75-year deficit (AARP 2005).

Much has been written about each of these approaches, and the purpose of this book is not to duplicate those analyses. Rather, it is to explore the experiences of countries that have systems much like that of the United States and have introduced equities into their public pension system in each of these three ways. This chapter summarizes the lessons learned both in terms of system design and the ability to manage the risk associated with equity investment.

THE CHALLENGE FACING THE UNITED STATES

By the end of the twentieth century, the United States had largely succeeded in providing its elderly, for the first time in history, a reasonably secure and comfortable standard of living.

This achievement has since been threatened by two developments. Rapid population aging most directly challenges the solvency of public pay-as-you-go programs. Employers have also withdrawn from the sponsorship of defined-benefit pension plans. Shifts in the nature of industry and increased regulation explain some of this withdrawal. But the financial storm at the end of the century, the combination of low interest rates (which increased liabilities) and a bear market (which eroded assets), hastened the demise of defined-benefit plans everywhere.

In the United States, employers have largely replaced defined-benefit plans with defined-contribution 401(k) plans. On the positive side, this shift eliminated severance incentives that used system resources to induce the "retirement" of workers who were clearly employable and not truly old, but critical shortcomings remain. Employer-sponsored defined-contribution plans were not designed to be the primary private-sector component of the nation's retirement income system. They are voluntary and transfer all the responsibility for retirement planning to the individual worker. They also expose participants to significant financial and longevity risks. They are costly to administer, and they tend to leak assets so that workers often arrive at retirement with insufficient balances.

In addition to the withdrawal of employers from the provision of retirement income, the nation's most pressing retirement income problem, as already noted, is the financial shortfall the Social Security system faces. While this shortfall is not enormous when viewed as a percentage of GDP, it will not be easily closed. The payroll tax, which funds both Social Security and Medicare, now takes more than 15 percent of earnings, split evenly between workers and employers. The benefit cuts enacted in 1983, which will be phased in over the first quarter of the twenty-first century, will reduce Social Security replacement rates to their lowest point in history. Given the substantial risks in 401(k) plans, further reductions in Social Security pensions could result in clearly inadequate old-age incomes. To restore solvency without a significant tax increase or cut in old-age incomes, many policymakers would add investments in equities to the program design.

To help evaluate the nation's options going forward, this book reviewed the experience of three nations with Anglo-Saxon retirement income systems similar to our own—the United Kingdom, Australia, and Canada. All three expanded their retirement income systems between 1965 and 1980. They broadened access to employer plan benefits and made these benefits more secure. They also expanded public pension programs using a two-tier design, a flat basic benefit and an earnings-related benefit, that replaced similar levels of preretirement earnings. In the United States, unlike the other three nations, the two tiers are contained within a single program—Social Security (see Table 7.1).

Since 1980, the United Kingdom, Australia, and Canada have each reformed their public old-age income programs along the lines of one of the approaches proposed by the Advisory Council: carve-out individual accounts, add-on individual accounts, and the investment of a portion of trust fund assets in equities. Each system is solvent in the sense that they are expected to pay benefits promised under current law, and the reforms have been in place long enough to illustrate the opportunities and challenges implicit in each.

Table 7.1 The Two-Part Structure of "Expanded" Anglo-Saxon Public Pension Programs

	Basic flat benefit		Earnings-related benefit	
Nation	Name	Type	Name	Type
United Kingdom	Basic State Pension	Social insurance; payroll-tax funded	State Earnings Related Pension Scheme (SERPS)	Social insurance; payroll-tax funded
Australia	Age Pension	Means-tested; general revenue funded	Superannuation Guarantee	Individual account; mandatory saving
Canada	Old Age Security	Demogrant; general revenue funded	Canada/Quebec Pension Plan (C/QPP)	Social insurance; payroll-tax funded
United States	Social Security (on earnings in first tier of benefit formula)	Social insurance; payroll-tax funded	Social Security (on earnings above first tier of benefit formula)	Social insurance; payroll-tax funded

LESSONS FROM THE UK EXPERIENCE

By the end of the 1970s, the United Kingdom had created a retirement income system quite similar to that in the United States. Its two social insurance programs, the flat Basic State Pension and SERPS, together would have produced benefits very close to those provided by the U.S. Social Security program. Britain also had a robust employer pension institution, similar to that in the United States. A major difference was that the British government allowed, indeed encouraged, employers to "contract out" of SERPS and provide the public earnings-related benefit through their equity-funded pension plan.

In response to a change of government in 1979 and to the growing awareness of the impending demographic transition, the United Kingdom reformed its system along the lines of the Advisory Council carve-out approach. It sharply cut public pensions, both the Basic State Pension and SERPS, and shifted an increasing portion of the government's diminished old-age income responsibilities to the private sector. Contracting out had already established the principal of private retirement plans assuming social security obligations, with those plans funded with contributions carved out of the payroll tax and invested in equities. The government now encouraged workers to contract out of SERPS using individual retirement savings accounts. At the same time, the government guaranteed Basic State Pension was falling to just 15 percent of the national average earnings by the end of the twentieth century and is projected to be just 7 percent by the middle of the twenty-first century.

British employers, like those in the United States, are also withdrawing from traditional defined-benefit plans. The departure came later in Britain and for somewhat different reasons. But, by the beginning of the twenty-first century, private sector employers are closing their defined-benefit plans to new workers and offering, at best, individual account programs where workers bear most of the funding responsibilities and all of the risks. Thus, the great majority of those who contract out of SERPS (roughly half the workforce) will soon be in individual account type programs. So, like American workers under a carve-out reform, British workers are increasingly dependent on sharply reduced government pensions and accumulations in individual retirement accounts.

The British experience illustrates the high cost of administering and regulating accounts carved out of the payroll tax. Most U.S. carve-out proposals would improve on the British design by using the government to collect and administer accounts with small balances. The cost

Table 7.2 Estimated Administrative Costs of Pension Systems and Their Effect on Assets at Retirement in the United States

Pension system	Annual administrative costs	Percent reduction in assets at retirement
Social Security	$11 per participant	2
Federal Thrift Savings Plan	$25 per participant	5
Mutual funds (average)	1.09% of assets	23
Private defined-contribution funds		
Large plans	$24 per participant 0.8% of assets	21
Small plans	$60 per participant 1% of assets	30

SOURCE: Congressional Budget Office (2003).

of selling and administering individual accounts, even well above the "small balance" threshold, is nevertheless high (Table 7.2). The British mis-selling scandal also illustrates costs created by the vulnerability of carve-out designs to abuse and error. The British experience also illustrates the difficulties carve-out designs encounter in defining regulatory rules on matters such as annuitization and inflation-proofing—difficulties that are costly to overcome.

Another lesson from the U.K experience is that the "adequacy" of old-age pensions is more of a "relative" than an "absolute" concept— that is, notions of adequacy are tied to a moving social norm, not a static basket of necessities. Britain price-indexed the Basic State Pension in 1980, in effect defining the basic pension as the basket of goods and services that could be purchased by the Basic State Pension in 1980, which was then 25 percent of average earnings. Britain's welfare system, however, had long pegged poverty as income less than about 20 percent of average earnings, a moving social norm. Both Conservative and Labor governments had used means-tested programs to assure the elderly an income above that threshold amount, pegged to incomes in the economy at large.

As British social insurance pensions declined, the only way to assure the elderly an adequate income was through a means-tested welfare program, but such programs reduce incentives to work and save. To counter the moral hazard created by means-testing, Britain introduced the Pension Credit with a tapered withdrawal rate. Because of the taper, half the elderly population became eligible for means-tested benefits. The proportion will rise as the Basic State Pension continues to decline relative to earnings, since the welfare benchmark keeps pace with earnings growth. By midcentury, three-quarters of the elderly should thus be eligible for means-tested benefits at any point in time and a greater proportion at some point in their lives. The British experience thus illustrates how means-tested programs can rapidly expand through the introduction of a taper designed to counteract moral hazard.

Guaranteed Social Security benefits are especially vulnerable to falling below socially acceptable norms and triggering an expansion of means-testing under a carve-out reform. In the first instance, carve-out proposals reduce Social Security benefits to fit within the program's current resources. Many carve-out proposals do this through price-indexing or some other mechanism that does not assure the elderly an income that will likely be seen as adequate. All carve-out proposals then allow workers to divert a portion of their social insurance contributions into an individual retirement savings account but require in exchange a reduction in their Social Security benefits. Even if a carve-out reform retains an adequate initial benefit, workers who elect the individual account option will generally bring their remaining guaranteed benefit well below the adequacy threshold. The only way to assure such workers an adequate income is through a means-tested program. The British experience suggests that a broad take-up of the individual account option, with a reduction in guaranteed benefits below the socially acceptable level of adequacy, could quickly lead to a major expansion of means-testing that could make the elderly, on the whole, a welfare-dependent population. To avoid this outcome, the British government is now considering major reform of its retirement income system that would abandon the carve-out design.

The carve-out approach as implemented in the United Kingdom produced sharply lower guaranteed social insurance benefits, the privatization of much of the nation's diminished retirement income system, increased reliance on individual retirement income planning, and a major expansion of means testing. The goal was to reduce dependence on the state and increase reliance on individual initiative and private financial markets. However, retirement income systems emerged throughout the industrial world because people generally proved themselves incapable of preparing for their own old age. Many people have a myopic view when trading consumption today for consumption in the future. In addition, many people simply lack the information and investment channels they need to accumulate and protect their savings for retirement. The British experience suggests that this original incapacity has not been overcome. If given the latitude, workers will save too little, mishandle the risks and complexities of retirement income planning, and require an extensive safety net. Thus, the outcome of sharp social insurance cutbacks and expanded privatization—in the United States as in Britain—is likely to be just the opposite of what its proponents desire.

LESSONS FROM THE AUSTRALIAN EXPERIENCE

Australia reformed its retirement income system somewhat along the lines of add-on individual accounts. Like the add-on proposal, the Australian Superannuation Guarantee program brought additional resources to the retirement income system. Superannuation Guarantee contributions, at 9 percent of earnings, are far larger than add-on proposals in the United States, but the preexisting Australian public system was limited to the means-tested Age Pension and had no earnings-related component. The addition of a substantial earnings-related Superannuation Guarantee was therefore needed to approximate the benefit structure in typical Anglo-Saxon retirement systems—that of contributions and benefits rising, and replacement rates falling, with earnings.

The administrative costs of the individual accounts under Australia's Superannuation Guarantee program are lower than those in the U.K individual account system because the contributions are largely collected and invested collectively, by employers or employer-union plans, and thus capture important economies of scale in marketing, administration, and investment management. The mandatory character of the contribution also reduces marketing, education, and operating costs below those in voluntary U.S. 401(k) programs, which are otherwise of comparable size and similarly managed.

Many Australians had hoped that workers would accumulate enough assets in their Superannuation Guarantee accounts to return the Age Pension to its original safety net function. But the Australian Treasury projections have 75 percent of the elderly collecting Age Pension benefits even after the Superannuation Guarantee program matures, with even more collecting benefits at some point in their lives. The retirement income generated by Superannuation Guarantee contributions also carries a good deal of risk. For this reason as well, the Age Pension will remain the central component of the Australian retirement income system. The continuing centrality of the Age Pension in the Australian system, even with the Superannuation Guarantee taking 9 percent of earnings, illustrates the high cost of retirement. By analogy, the standard contribution to U.S. 401(k) plans, which is also 9 percent, (ProfitSharing/401(k) Council of America 2005) will never accumulate enough assets to serve as the sole source of support in retirement, highlighting the need for a meaningful Social Security benefit.

A key lesson for the United States arises from the interaction between Australia's Superannuation Guarantee individual account and its means-tested Age Pension programs. The means-tested Age Pension plays an important role in that it offsets a significant portion of the risk associated with equity investments in the Superannuation Guarantee program. Age Pension benefits rise for those who outlive their assets, invest poorly, or are in unlucky cohorts when it comes to investment returns. It also funds those higher benefits by reducing benefits to those who do well. The means-tested Age Pension therefore functions as a valuable risk-pooling mechanism.

The interaction between Australia's individual account and means-tested programs also has two dysfunctional effects. The first is the over-investment in assets such as housing, consumer durables, and exotic annuity products that yield lower returns than alternative investments (such as stocks and bonds issued by the business sector) on a before-tax and before-Age Pension basis, but higher returns after netting out tax and Age-Pension reductions. Potentially far more serious is the incentive for workers to retire early, cut back on savings, and spend down their assets prior to reaching old age, so that they can collect a higher Age Pension benefit. In other words, the Age Pension means test creates a powerful incentive for workers to retire early and dissipate assets well before they reach "old age." By contrast, the incentives in the 401(k) program and the actuarial adjustment of U.S. Social Security benefits both reward continued work. These incentives increase the resources of the retirement income system and encourage workers to delay drawing down their Social Security and private retirement wealth and shift it to older ages. Should the United States move to a means-tested public program, whether to manage risk or better target public support for the elderly, it could undo key work incentives and weaken the nation's retirement income system.

LESSONS FROM THE CANADIAN EXPERIENCE

Canada reformed its pension system, in response to the pressures created by demographic transition, by raising taxes to prefund the public program and investing a portion of social insurance trust fund assets in equities. The cost of administering and managing equity investments through a centrally managed trust fund is significantly lower than in a myriad of individual accounts. Investment and mortality risks are also pooled far more effectively. The main disadvantage of this approach is the potential interference of the federal government in private corporate activity.

While equity investments bring a higher expected rate of return than bonds, they are also risky. The question is the extent to which individuals face this market risk under an individual account arrangement as opposed to investing through the trust fund. Given the enormous variation in stock market returns, a constant contribution rate in an individual account program will inevitably produce substantial overfunding relative to the target replacement rate for some cohorts and substantial underfunding for others. Attempts to stabilize replacement rates would require constant tinkering with contribution rates and can at best be only partially successful. Thus, it is virtually impossible to ensure stable replacement rates when individuals must rely on their independent investment results.

In the case of the trust fund investing in equities, individuals avoid most of the market risk. They do not have to cash out their holdings at any particular time, but rather receive the earnings-related benefit defined by the program. If the market falls and the plan is judged to be out of balance, Canada would adjust CPP contribution and benefit levels to restore solvency over a period of 100 years. In other words, the trust fund functions as a shock absorber, dampening the volatility inherent in equity investment.

Future stock returns, of course, could turn out to be considerably lower than those experienced in the past. Such a decline, however, would be far more disruptive if the equities were held in individual accounts. In both cases, resources would be inadequate to finance projected retirement income benefits. The question is who would bear the loss. With individual accounts, retirees would simply have to live with lower benefits. With trust fund investments, younger taxpayers could be required to pay higher taxes to offset some or all of the shortfall. The automatic stabilizer in the CPP would trigger a combination of benefit cuts and tax increases that would return the program to balance over a 100-year period. Incorporating equity investments within a public defined-benefit pension framework thus dramatically reduces the risk faced by future retirees compared to what they would face with individual accounts.

The major concern about investing social insurance trust fund assets in equities is the power it potentially puts in the hands of government. Using trust fund assets for "socially desirable" purposes could undermine retirement income security. It would also open the door to government interference in the economy—often without public oversight—and this, in turn, undermines the democratic process.[1] To guard against such threats, Canada has adopted a well-thought-out design, taken from the governance of employer-defined pension plans, intended to minimize political interference in the management of trust fund investments. The Canadian structure calls for an independent CPPIB, which is selected through a laborious political process that involves a wide array of provincial and federal officials. The board must periodically review its own performance and make frequent and extensive reports to the pubic. Within this governance framework, the board is free to invest trust fund assets in the full gamut of opportunities available to employer defined-benefit pension fund managers.

In the United States, most proposals for investing Social Security trust fund assets in equities reject such an active investment policy. They instead call for a passive strategy that invests trust fund assets in a broad market index, such as the Russell 3000 or the Wilshire 5000. (Note that in most individual account proposals, the government would also be required to select a series of funds that could be used in the program.) An expert investment board would select the index, choose portfolio managers for the accounts, and monitor the performance of the managers. To ensure that government ownership does not disrupt corporate governance, most proposals require that voting rights be given to the asset managers, not voted at all, or voted in the same fashion as the other shareholders, which is equivalent to not voting at all.

Two types of government pensions in the United States already invest in equities with no apparent ill effects. The federal Thrift Savings Plan for government employees has established highly efficient stock index funds. That is, the government is responsible for selecting the investment options provided to government employees. To date, these decisions have not been influenced by politics. The plan's designers insulated investment decisions by setting up an independent investment board, narrowing investment choices, and requiring strict fiduciary duties. The plan also operates in a political culture of noninterference. Its creators made clear from the beginning that economic, not social or political, goals were to be the sole purpose of the investment board.

State and local pension funds also invest in equities. Some opponents of trust fund investment in equities contend that state and local pensions interfere in private sector activities. The contention is that these funds often undertake investments that achieve political or social goals, divest stocks to demonstrate that they do not support some perceived immoral or unethical behavior, and interfere with corporate activity by voting proxies and other activities. Recent research, however, documents that political considerations have had almost no effect on investment decisions at the state and local level (Munnell and Sundén 2001). Indeed, public pension plans appear to be performing as well as private plans.

The political stakes in placing such a large amount of wealth and corporate shares in government hands would still be high. But the task of overseeing equity investments in Social Security would be simplified, and the likelihood of success significantly enhanced, if it were done through the trust fund. The task of governing the investment of the trust fund in a passive equity index is clearly less than the daunting challenge of overseeing and regulating equity investments in a myriad of individual accounts.

SUMMARY

The previous survey reveals three important conclusions relating to the size of benefits, the cost of retirement income programs, and the ability to manage investment risk.

The Size of Benefits

Workers presumably want an old-age income sufficient to maintain their standard of living. Social security, like public retirement income programs in other Anglo-Saxon nations, has never explicitly targeted this objective. The primary goal has been to provide reasonably adequate earnings replacement for low-wage workers and a base upon which publicly subsidized and regulated employer plans, plus other private saving efforts, could deliver reasonably adequate earnings replacement for middle- and upper-income earners. This combination of Social Security, employer plans, and private saving (primarily the accumulation of home equity) succeeded in delivering reasonably comfortable retirements to much of the elderly population by the end of the twentieth century.

This achievement will be difficult for Social Security to maintain going forward. As noted, Social Security replacement rates will decline under current law as the Normal Retirement Age increases, as ever larger Medicare premiums are deducted from Social Security checks, and as more benefits are subject to the personal income tax.

If wages grow as projected, benefits will decline relative to preretirement earnings but will rise in "real terms"—that is, they will allow beneficiaries to purchase a larger basket of goods and services. A key question is therefore whether adequacy of Social Security benefits should be defined in absolute or relative terms. The experience in the three nations reviewed suggests that adequacy is, in large measure, relative. Australia's Age Pension guarantees the elderly an income equal to 25 percent of male average earnings, or about a third of the national average wage. The Canadian Guaranteed Security Income program sets a similar minimum income floor. Britain, in 1980, fixed the Basic State Pension in absolute terms by price-indexing the benefit. When the Basic State Pension fell below the nation's welfare stipend, traditionally set at about 20 percent of national average earnings, Britain transformed its retirement income system to assure the elderly that minimal welfare-level income. To do so, it effectively replaced the Basic State Pension with the Pension Credit as the government's "basic" retirement income program, replacing social insurance with means-tested welfare. Given that many U.S. proposals for reforming Social Security include further benefit cuts, the British experience, in particular, suggests that defining the minimum public pension—and whether it should be absolute or relative and guaranteed or means tested—are critical agenda items.

It also seems appropriate to identify some intermediate income target—between just above poverty and the maintenance of preretirement living standards—as a viable objective for Social Security or for the system as a whole. The most common such intermediate benchmark is a "modest but adequate" standard of living, defined as an income that "affords full opportunity to participate in contemporary society and the basic options it offers" (Parker 2002). For individuals, 40 percent of the average wage, the traditional Social Security replacement rate, is a reasonable income target needed to achieve that "modest but adequate" benchmark. The nation should seriously consider what it would take to assure this level of old-age income.

The Cost of Benefits

Retirement income programs are expensive. At the most basic level, the cost is measured by the required contributions. Social Security old-age and survivor benefits take 10.6 percent of covered earnings, split evenly between employer and employee. They require another 2.02 percent to fund promised benefits over the next 75 years and 3.70 percent to fund benefits over the infinite horizon. Standard 401(k) contributions run about 9 percent of earnings—6 percent from the worker and a 3 percent employer match. Total contributions for someone who makes the standard 401(k) contribution are nearly 20 percent of earnings.[2] A full accounting of the costs of retirement income programs would also include government tax expenditures—the foregone government revenue resulting from the special tax treatment given to pensions.

The current payroll tax, 10.6 percent for old age and survivor benefits and 15.3 percent including disability insurance and Medicare, though low by continental European standards, is high relative to payroll taxes in Australia and Canada. Most Americans already pay more in payroll tax than they do in income tax, and there is significant political resistance to raising the rate.[3]

Canada did increase its payroll tax in its 1997 reform. But the levy had been low, and the rate was pushed to only 9.9 percent. Australia also imposed mandatory contributions to individual "Superannuation Guarantee" accounts, akin to a tax on earnings, but the required contribution was only 9 percent. This experience suggests there may be limited resistance to extracting contributions up to about 10 percent of earnings, but it becomes significantly more difficult to raise rates past the U.S. level of 15 percent. If the United States wants to add revenues to its programs for the elderly, it may well have to turn to sources other than the payroll tax.[4]

Managing Risk of Equity Investment

Because the taxes for financing public retirement systems are so high and benefits are scheduled to increase rapidly as the population ages, nearly all countries have attempted to mitigate some of the projected burden by introducing equities into their public pension systems.

The extent to which an entity can "count on" the higher returns of equity investments depends on its ability to manage the risk. Workers who need to annuitize accumulations in an individual account at a particular date are not well-positioned to manage the risk in equities. Defined-benefit plans which can pool the risks for large numbers of people and spread risks over time are positioned far better. But, as the experiences in the United States, the United Kingdom, and Canada illustrate, employer-sponsored defined-benefit plans were not able to emerge unscathed from the "perfect storm" of the simultaneous collapse of interest rates and equity prices at the turn of the century.

The best way to manage risk, as the Canadian example illustrates, is to hold equities in the social security trust fund. This approach is better for two reasons. First, the trust fund, unlike individual workers, can be expected to use professional investment management that can reduce risk without sacrificing returns. Second, the infinite-horizon Social Security fund can smooth fluctuations in returns across time, so the adjustments in work or consumption potentially required of any one cohort would be dramatically lower.

On balance, it seems like investing a portion of the social security trust fund in equities is a feasible and desirable strategy. The higher expected returns would moderate the tax increases and benefits cuts required to close the financing gap. The approach has its limitations. Many observers agree that it would be undesirable for the trust fund to hold more than 5 to 10 percent of total U.S. equities. If in 2005 40 percent of the Social Security trust funds ($1.9 trillion) were invested in equities, trust fund holdings ($0.4 \times \$1.9$ trillion = $760 billion) would amount to only 4 percent of total equities outstanding ($19 trillion). A policy of investing 40 percent of the trust fund in equities, phased in between 2006 and 2018, assuming a 6.5 percent real rate of return on equities, would eliminate more than half of Social Security's 75-year deficit. The question is how much political turmoil would such a strategy create and whether the gains are worth it.

CONCLUSION

At some point, the debate over retirement income policy stops dealing in the pragmatics of costs, benefits, and efficiency. Proponents of benefit reductions and carve-out individual accounts often present their proposals as part of a larger transition to an "ownership society," with individual households shaking free of Social Security and becoming far more self-reliant. This vision expresses a notion of the "good society," an end in itself, and a belief that the vitality of the nation derives from the activity of independent, freestanding households.

The notions of "social security" and even a "national retirement income system" derive from a different conception of the "good society" and the source of national vitality. This vision, which your authors hold, has a far less sanguine view of the state of nature. It sees individual households as immersed in the demands of everyday life and too myopic to closely negotiate the powerful cross currents of modern industrial economies. It sees saving for retirement as a complex matter, difficult to understand and fraught with uncertainties. Those who hold this vision claim that paring down Social Security and substituting individual accounts is simply too perilous, while preserving social security, broadly construed, enhances independence and allows full participation in the life of society.

This is not the place to evaluate these larger claims regarding the effects of Social Security and national retirement income systems. Both perspectives have elements of truth, and both can be extended too far. The point is that such beliefs underlie much of the retirement income debate. As such, they need to be acknowledged and discussed. But they must also be held somewhat in check, as we have a serious pragmatic problem that must be solved. Indeed, the process of developing a practical response might help the nation resolve this broader political debate.

Notes

1. Note, however, that investing trust fund assets in equities forecloses the opportunity to use these assets as a captive source of credit for the government, which typically results in the government spending more than it otherwise would.
2. Including the employer's Social Security contribution and 401(k) match in the worker's earnings, the contribution is about 18 percent of earnings.
3. There is less resistance to raising the cap on the wage base or on forcing all new state and local workers into the system, and the 1994–1996 Advisory Council generally agreed on including these measures in any reform package.
4. General government revenues are drawn from a far broader base than the payroll tax, giving government the ability to spread the burden of population aging and raise taxes that produce the least adverse effects. General revenue financing also allows the government to redirect resources freed up by population aging and low labor-force growth, such as expenditures on education and additional public infrastructure, buildings, and equipment.

References

AARP. 2005. *Reimagining America: AARP's Blueprint for the Future*. Washington, DC: AARP. http://assets.aarp.org/www.aarp.org_/articles/legpolicy/blueprint200508.pdf (accessed March 9, 2006).

Achenbaum, W. Andrew. 1978. *Old Age in the New Land: The American Experience since 1790*. Baltimore: Johns Hopkins University Press.

Ackerloff, George. 1982. "Labor Contracts as Partial Gift Exchange." *Quarterly Journal of Economics* 97(2): 543–569.

Ambachtsheer, Keith. 1996. "Moving to a Fiduciary CPP Investment Policy: Two Possible Paths." Paper prepared for the federal-provincial Working Group on CPP Investment Policy.

———. 2000. "Public Pension Fund Power in Canada: For Good . . . or For Evil?" *Canada Investment Review* 13(2): 12–17.

Andrews, Emily S. 1985. *The Changing Profile of Pensions in America*. Washington, DC: Employee Benefits Research Institute.

Arrow, Kenneth J., and Robert C. Lind. 1970. "Uncertainty and the Evaluation of Public Investment Decisions." *American Economic Review* 60(2): 364–378.

Australian Bureau of Statistics. 2004. "Retirement and Retirement Intentions, Australia." Cat. no. 6238.0. Available at http://www.abs.gov.au/Ausstats/abs@.nsf/lookupMF/3DC3297FAA3CB8ABCA2568A90013938A (accessed February 6, 2006).

Ball, Robert M. 1947. "Social Insurance and the Right to Assistance." *The Social Service Review* 21(3). Reprinted in *Insuring the Essentials: Bob Ball on Social Security*, Thomas N. Bethell, ed. 2000. The Century Foundation, pp. 33–51.

Bateman, Hazel, and John Piggott. 1997. "Private Pensions in OECD Countries: Australia." OECD Labour Market and Social Policy Occasional Paper no. 23. Paris: Organisation for Economic Co-operation and Development.

———. 2001a. "Australia's Mandatory Retirement Saving Policy: A View from the New Millennium. Pension Reform Primer." Electronic Discussion Paper 4 (August). Sydney: Center for Applied Economic Research, University of New South Wales.

———. 2001b. "The Australian Approach to Retirement Income Provision." Paper prepared for the International Seminar on Social Security Pensions, held in Tokyo, March 5–7.

Battle, Ken. 2003. *Sustaining Public Pensions in Canada: A Tale of Two Reforms*. Ottawa: Caledon Institute of Social Policy.

Béland, Daniel. Forthcoming. "The Politics of Social Learning: Finance, Institutions and Pension Reform in the United States and Canada." *Governance: An International Journal of Policy, Administration and Institutions.*

Béland, Daniel, and John Myles. 2005. "Stasis Amidst Change: Canadian Pension Reform in an Age of Retrenchment." In *Ageing and Pension Reform Around the World*, Giuliano Bonoli and Toshimitsu Shinkawa, eds. Cheltenham: Edward Elgar, pp. 252–273.

Biggs, Andrew. 2002. Testimony before the Senate Finance Committee Hearing on the Final Report Produced by The President's Commission to Strengthen Social Security. http://www.socialsecurity.org/pubs/testimony/ct-ab100302 .pdf (accessed March 9, 2006).

Blake, David. 2000. "Two Decades of Pension Reform in the UK: What Are the Implications for Occupational Pension Schemes?" Discussion paper PI-0004. London: Pensions Institute, Birkbeck College, University of London.

———. 2002. "The United Kingdom Pension System: Key Issues." Discussion paper PI-0107. London: Pensions Institute, Birkbeck College, University of London.

Blake, David, and John Board. 2000. "Measuring Value Added in the Pensions Industry." *Geneva Papers on Risk and Insurance* 25(4): 539–567.

Blake, David, and J. Michael Orszag. 1997. *Towards a Universal Funded Second Pension.* London: Pensions Institute, Birkbeck College, University of London.

Blake, David, and John Turner. 2005. *Voluntary Carve Outs for Social Security Reform: Lessons from the United Kingdom.* Washington, DC: AARP Public Policy Institute.

Bodie, Zvi. 2001. "Financial Engineering and Social Security Reform." In *Risk Aspects of Investment-Based Social Security Reform*, John Y. Campbell and Martin Feldstein, eds. Chicago: University of Chicago Press, pp. 193–227.

Bohn, Henning. 1997. "Social Security Reform and Financial Markets." In *Social Security Reform: Links to Saving, Investment, and Growth*, Steven A. Sass and Robert K. Triest, eds. Boston: Federal Reserve Bank of Boston, pp. 193–227.

Bovbjerg, Barbara D. 2003. "Private Pensions: Changing Funding Rules and Enhancing Incentives Can Improve Plan Funding." GAO-04-176T. Washington, DC: U.S. General Accounting Office. http://www.gao.gov/new .items/d04176t.pdf (accessed March 10, 2006).

Brown, Claire. 1994. *American Standards of Living, 1918–1988.* Cambridge, MA: Blackwell.

Buessing, Marric, and Mauricio Soto. 2006. "The State of Private Pensions: Current 5500 Data." *Issue in Brief* 52. Chestnut Hill, MA: Center for Retirement Research at Boston College.

Bureau of Labor Statistics. 2005. *Labor Force Statistics from the Current Population Survey*. http://www.bls.gov/cps/ (accessed August 24, 2006).

Burtless, Gary, and Joseph Quinn. 2002. "Is Working Longer the Answer for an Aging Workforce?" *Issue in Brief* 11. Chestnut Hill, MA: Center for Retirement Research at Boston College.

Canada Pension Plan (CPP). 1997. *Securing the Canada Pension Plan: Agreement on Proposed Changes to the CPP*. Ottawa: Canadian Department of Finance. http://www.fin.gc.ca/cpp/inedex.html (accessed March 9, 2006).

Canada Pension Plan Investment Board (CPPIB). 1997. *Canada Pension Plan Investment Board Act*. Ottawa: Canadian Department of Finance. http://lois.justice.gc.ca/en/C-8.3/ (accessed March 9, 2006).

———. 2003. *Annual Report of the Canada Pension Plan Investment Board*. Toronto: CPPIB.

———. 2005. *Annual Report of the Canada Pension Plan Investment Board*. Toronto: CPPIB.

Canadian Department of Justice. 2004. *Air Canada Pension Plan Solvency Deficiency Funding Regulations.* http://laws.justice.gc.ca/en/P-7.01/SOR-2004-174/ (accessed May 18, 2005).

Centrelink. 2005. *How Much Age Pension Do I Get?* Manuka, Australia: Department of Human Services. http://www.centrelink.gov.au/internet/internet.nsf/payments /pay_how_agepens.htm (accessed March 9, 2006).

Chandler, A.D. 1977. *The Visible Hand: The Managerial Revolution in American Business*. Cambridge, MA: Harvard University Press.

———. 1990. *Scale and Scope: The Dynamics of Industrial Capitalism*. Cambridge, MA: Harvard University Press.

Clark, Tom. 2001. "Recent Pensions Policy and the Pension Credit." IFS Briefing Note no. 17. London: Institute for Fiscal Studies.

———. 2002. "Reward for Saving and Alleviating Poverty? The Final Pension Credit Proposals." IFS Briefing Note no. 22. London: Institute for Fiscal Studies.

Clark, Tom, and Carl Emmerson. 2002. "The Tax and Benefit System and the Decision to Invest in a Stakeholder Pension." IFS Briefing Note no. 28. London: Institute for Fiscal Studies. http://www.ifs.org.uk/publications/briefnotes.shtml (accessed March 9, 2006).

———. 2003. "Privatising Provision and Attacking Poverty? The Direction of UK Pension Policy under New Labor." *Journal of Pension Economics and Finance* 2(1): 67–89.

Committee on Economic Security. 1935. "Report to the President of the Committee on Economic Security." Table 17. Washington, DC: Committee on Economic Security.

Commonwealth Treasury of Australia. 2001. "Towards Higher Retirement

Incomes for Australians: A History of the Australian Retirement Income System since Federation." In *Economic Roundup Centenary Edition 2001.* Canberra, Australia: Commonwealth of Australia, pp. 65–92.

———. 2002. "Inquiry into Superannuation and Standards of Living in Retirement—Submission by the Commonwealth Treasury." In *Economic Roundup Winter 2002.* Canberra, Australia: Commonwealth of Australia, pp. 1–44.

Congressional Budget Office. 2003. *The Baby Boomers' Retirement Prospects: An Overview.* Washington, DC: Congressional Budget Office.

———. 2004. *Administrative Costs of Private Accounts in Social Security.* Washington, DC: Congressional Budget Office.

Cooke, Murray. 2003. "The Canada Pension Plan Goes to Market." *Canada Review of Social Policy* 51(Spring/Summer): 126–131. http://www.yorku .ca/crsp/issue51/issue51-10.pdf (accessed March 9, 2006).

Costa, Dora. 1998. *The Evolution of Retirement: An American Economic History, 1880–1990.* Chicago: University of Chicago Press.

Coward, Laurence E. 1995. *Private Pensions in OECD Countries: Canada.* Paris: Organisation for Economic Co-operation and Development.

Davis, E. Phillip. 1997. "Private Pensions in OECD Countries—the United Kingdom." Labour Market and Social Policy Occasional Paper no. 21. Paris: Organisation of Economic Co-operation and Development.

———. 2000. "Regulation of Private Pensions—A Case Study of the UK." Discussion Paper PI-0009. London: Pensions Institute, Birkbeck College, University of London.

———. 2003. "Is There A Pension Crisis in the UK?" Draft keynote address for the Japan Pension Research Council meeting, held in Tokyo, September 18–19.

Daykin, Chris. 2001. "Contracting Out: A Partnership Between Public and Private Pensions." *Pensions Management Institute News* (July): 1–3.

DeWitt, Larry. 1999. "The History and Development of the Social Security Retirement Earnings Income Test." Special Study 7 by the SSA Historian's Office. Washington, DC: Social Security Administration.

Diamond, Peter. 1997. "Macroeconomic Aspects of Social Security Reform." *Brookings Papers on Economic Activity* (2): 1–66.

Diamond, Peter, and Peter Orszag. 2004. *Social Security Reform: A Balanced Approach.* Washington, DC: Brookings Institution.

Edey, Malcolm, and John Simon. 1996. "Australia's Retirement Income System: Implications for Saving and Capital Markets." NBER Working Paper no. 5799. Cambridge, MA: National Bureau of Economic Research.

Emmerson, Carl. 2002. "Pension Reform in the United Kingdom: Increasing the Role of Private Pensions?" Paper prepared for the Pension Security in the 21st Century conference, held at the University of Oxford, March 8.

Esping-Andersen, Gosta. 1990. *Three Worlds of Welfare Capitalism*. Princeton, NJ: Princeton University Press.

Federal Interagency Forum on Aging-Related Statistics. 2004. *Older Americans 2004: Key Indicators of Well-Being*. Washington, DC: U.S. Government Printing Office.

Federal, Provincial and Territorial Governments of Canada. 1996a. "An Information Paper for Consultations on the Canada Pension Plan." Ottawa: Canadian Department of Finance.

———. 1996b. *Report on the Canada Pension Plan Consultations*. Ottawa: Canadian Department of Finance.

Fields, Gary S., and Olivia S. Mitchell. 1984. "The Effects of Social Security Reforms on Retirement Ages and Retirement Incomes." NBER Working Paper no. W1348. Cambridge, MA: National Bureau of Economic Research.

Fisher, Gordon. 1995. "Is There Such a Thing as an Absolute Poverty Line Over Time? Evidence from the United States, Britain, Canada, and Australia on the Income Elasticity of the Poverty Line." Poverty Measurement Working Paper. Washington, DC: U.S. Census Bureau. http://www.census .gov/hhes/poverty/povmeas/papers/elastap4.html#C10 (accessed March 9, 2006).

Friedberg, Leora, and Anthony Webb. 2005. "Retirement and the Evolution of Pension Structure." *Journal of Human Resources* 40(2): 281–308.

Geanakoplos, John, Olivia S. Mitchell, and Stephen Zeldes. 2002. "Private Accounts, Prefunding, and Equity Investment under Social Security." In *Policies for an Aging Society*, A. Altman and David Shactman, eds. Baltimore: Johns Hopkins University Press, pp. 266–292.

Glasson, William H. 1918. *History of Military Pension Legislation of the United States*. New York: Oxford University Press.

Graebner, William. 1980. *A History of Retirement*. New Haven, CT: Yale University Press.

Gustman, Alan, and Thomas Steinmeier. 1992. "The Stampede toward Defined Contribution Pension Plans: Fact or Fiction?" *Industrial Relations* 31(2): 361–369.

HM Revenue and Customs. 2004. REV BN 39: Simplification Of The Taxation Of Pensions. London. http://www.hmrc.gov.uk/budget2004/revbn39 .htm (accessed July 26, 2006).

Hannah, Leslie. 1986. *Inventing Retirement: The Development of Occupational Pensions in Britain*. Cambridge: Cambridge University Press.

Hustead, Edwin C. 1998. "Trends in Retirement Income Plan Administrative Expenses." In *Living with Defined Contribution Pension: Remaking Responsibility for Retirement*, Olivia S. Mitchell and Sylvester J. Screiber, eds. Philadelphia: University of Pennsylvania Press, pp. 166–177.

Ibbotson Associates. 2003. *Stocks, Bonds, Bills, and Inflation 2003 Yearbook.* Chicago: Ibbotson Associates.

Ippolito, Richard. 1995. "Toward Explaining the Growth of Defined Contribution Plans." *Industrial Relations* 34(1): 1–19.

———. 1998. *Pension Plans and Employee Performance.* Chicago: University of Chicago Press.

King, Anthony, Agnes Walker, and Ann Harding. 1999. "Social Security, Aging, and Income Distribution in Australia." Paper prepared for the International Conference on Family, Social Policy and Financial Strategy, held in Taipei, April 16–17.

Kotlikoff, Laurence J., and David A. Wise. 1987. "The Incentive Effects of Private Pension Plans." In *Issues in Pension Economics*, Zvi Bodie, John B. Shoven, and David A. Wise, eds. Chicago: University of Chicago Press, pp. 283–336.

———. 1989. "Employee Retirement and a Firm's Pension Plan." In *The Economics of Aging*, David A. Wise, ed. Chicago: University of Chicago Press, pp. 279–330.

Lazear, Edward P. 1979. "Why is There Mandatory Retirement?" *Journal of Political Economy* 87(6): 1261–1284.

———. 1985. "Incentive Effects of Pensions." In *Pensions, Labor, and Individual Choice*, David A. Wise, ed. Chicago: University of Chicago Press, pp. 253–282.

Le Pan, Nicholas. 2003. Testimony to the House of Commons Standing Committee on Transport, Regarding the Regulation and Supervision of Air Canada's Pension Plans. Ottawa: Office of the Superintendent of Financial Institutions. http://www.osfi-bsif.gc.ca/app/DocRepository/1/eng/issues/ac/2003-04-04_e.pdf (accessed March 9, 2006).

Liu, Lillian. 1999. "Retirement Income Security in the United Kingdom." *Social Security Bulletin* 62(1): 1–23.

MaCurdy, Thomas, and John Shoven. 2001. "Asset Allocation and Risk Allocation: Can Social Security Improve Its Future Solvency by Investing in Private Securities?" In *Risk Aspects of Investment–Based Social Security Reform*, John Campbell and Martin Feldstein, eds. Chicago: Chicago University Press, pp. 11–32.

Maddison, Angus. 1995. *Monitoring the World Economy 1820–1992.* Paris: Organisation for Economic Co-operation and Development.

Margo, Robert A. 1991. "The Labor Force Participation of Older Americans in 1900: Further Results." NBER Working Paper Series on Historical Factors in Long Run Growth no. 27. Cambridge, MA: National Bureau of Economic Research.

Massachusetts Commission on Old-Age Pensions. 1909. "Preliminary Report,

Submitted to the Legislature in January." Boston: Massachusetts Commission on Old-Age Pensions.

Mehra, Rajnish, and Edward C. Prescott. 1985. "The Equity Premium: A Puzzle." *Journal of Monetary Economics* 15(2): 145–161.

Mendelson, Michael. 2005. *Financing the Canada and Quebec Pension Plans.* Washington, DC: AARP Public Policy Institute.

Milliman Consultants and Actuaries. 2005. *Milliman 2005 Pension Study.* n.p.

Mitchell, Daniel J., and Robert P. O'Quinn. 1997. "Australia's Privatized Retirement System: Lessons for the United States." *Backgrounder* no. 1149. Washington, DC: Heritage Foundation.

Moen, Jon. 1987. "Essays on the Labor Force and Labor Force Participation Rates: The United States from 1960 through 1950." PhD dissertation, University of Chicago.

Munnell, Alicia H. 1982. *The Economics of Private Pensions.* Washington, DC: Brookings Institution.

———. 2003. "The Declining Role of Social Security." *Just the Facts* no. 6. Chestnut Hill, MA: Center for Retirement Research at Boston College.

———. 2004. "Population Aging: It's Not Just The Baby Boom." *Issue in Brief* no.16. Chestnut Hill, MA: Center for Retirement Research at Boston College. http://www.bc.edu/centers/crr/issues/ib_16.pdf (accessed March 9, 2006).

Munnell, Alicia H., and Mauricio Soto. 2005a. "What Replacement Rates Do Households Actually Experience in Retirement?" Working paper no. 2005-10. Chestnut Hill, MA: Center for Retirement Research at Boston College.

———. 2005b. "How Do Pensions Affect Replacement Rates?" *Issue in Brief* no. 37. Chestnut Hill, MA: Center for Retirement Research at Boston College.

Munnell, Alicia H., and Annika Sundén. 2001. "Investment Practices of State and Local Pension Plans." In *Pensions in the Public Sector*, Olivia S. Mitchell and Edwin C. Hustead, eds. Philadelphia: University of Pennsylvania Press, pp. 153–194.

———. 2004. *Coming Up Short: The Challenge of 401(k) Plans.* Washington, DC: Brookings Institution.

Munnell, Alicia H., Annika Sundén, and Elizabeth Lidstone. 2002. "How Important Are Private Pensions?" *Issue in Brief* no. 8. Chestnut Hill, MA: Center for Retirement Research at Boston College.

Munnell, Alicia H., Robert K. Triest, and Natalia A. Jivan. 2004. "How Do Pensions Affect Actual and Expected Retirement Ages?" Working paper no. 2004-27. Chestnut Hill, MA: Center for Retirement Research at Boston College.

Murthi, Mamta, J. Michael Orszag, and Peter G. Orszag. 1999. "The Charge

Ratio on Individual Accounts: Lessons from the UK Experience." Birkbeck College Working paper no. 99-02. London: University of London.

Myles, John. 2000. "The Maturation of Canada's Retirement Income System: Income Levels, Income Inequality and Low Income among Older Persons." *Canadian Journal on Aging* 19(3): 287–316.

National Commission on Social Security Reform. 1983. *Report of the National Commission on Social Security Reform*. Washington, DC: Social Security Administration. http://www.ssa.gov/history/reports/gspan.html (accessed March 9, 2006).

Nobles, Richard. 2000. "Retirement Pensions in the United Kingdom." Report prepared for the XVI World Congress of Labour Law and Social Security, held in Jerusalem, September 3–7.

Office of the Chief Actuary. 2004. *21st Actuarial Report on the Canada Pension*. Ottawa: Canadian Department of Finance.

Organisation for Economic Co-operation and Development (OECD). 2003. Labour Market Statistics. Paris: Organisation for Economic Co-operation and Development.

Osberg, Lars. 2001. "Poverty Among Senior Citizens: A Canadian Success Story in International Perspective." LIS working paper no. 274. Differdange, Luxembourg: Luxembourg Income Study.

Palacios, Robert. 2002. "Managing Public Pension Reserves Part II: Lessons from Five OECD Initiatives." Social Protection Discussion Paper 0219. Washington, DC: World Bank.

Parker, Hermione, ed. 2002. *Modest but Adequate: A Reasonable Living Standard for Households Aged 65–74 Years*. London: Age Concern England. http://ww.york.ac.uk/res/fbu/documents/ageconcernmodad2002.pdf (accessed March 9, 2006).

Pelling, Margaret. 1991. "Old Age, Poverty and Disability in Norwich." In *Life, Death and the Elderly*, Margaret Pelling and Richard M. Smith, eds. London: Routledge, pp. 74–101.

Pensions Policy Institute (PPI). 2003. *The Pensions Landscape*. London: Pensions Policy Institute.

Pesando, James. 2001. "The Canada Pension Plan: Looking Back at the Recent Reforms." In *The State of Economics in Canada: Festschrift in Honour of David Slater*, Patrick Grady and Andrew Sharpe, eds. Ottawa: McGill-Queen's University Press, pp. 137–150.

Phipps, Shelley, and Lori Curtis. 2000. "Poverty and Child Well-Being in Canada and the United States: Does it Matter How We Measure Poverty?" Final report. Gatineau, Quebec, Canada: Human Resources Development Canada. http://www.hrsdc.gc.ca/en/cs/sp/sdc/pkrf/publications/research/2000-001273/2000-001273.pdf (accessed March 10, 2006).

Profit Sharing/401(k) Council of America. 2005. *48th Annual Survey of Profit Sharing and 401(k) Plans*. Chicago: Profit Sharing/401(k) Council of America.

Raphael, Marios. 1964. *Pensions and Public Servants: A Study of the Origins of the British System*. Paris: Mouton.

Rein, Martin, and John Turner. 2001. "Public-Private Interactions: Mandatory Pensions in Australia, the Netherlands, and Switzerland." *Review of Population and Social Policy* 10: 107–153.

Ross, David P., Katherine J. Scott, and Peter J. Smith. 2000. *The Canadian Fact Book on Poverty*. Ottawa: Canadian Council on Social Development.

Samwick, Andrew. 1998. "New Evidence on Pensions, Social Security, and the Timing of Retirement." *Journal of Public Economics* 70(2): 207–236.

Sarney, Mark, and Amy M. Preneta. 2001–2002. "The Canada Pension Plan's Experience with Investing Its Portfolio in Equities." *Social Security Bulletin* 64(2): 46–56.

Sass, Steven. 1997. *The Promise of Private Pensions*. Cambridge, MA: Harvard University Press.

———. 2003. "Reforming the UK Retirement System: Privatization Plus a Safety Net." *Issue in Brief* no. 3. Chestnut Hill, MA: Center for Retirement Research at Boston College. http://www.bc.edu/centers/crr/gib_3.shtml (accessed April 10, 2006).

Seager, Henry R. 1910. *Social Insurance: A Program of Social Reform*. New York: Macmillan.

Skolnik, Alfred M. 1976. "Private Pensions Plans, 1950–74." *Social Security Bulletin* 39(6): 3–17.

Slater, David W. 1997a. *The Pension Squeeze: The Impact of the March 1996 Federal Budget*. Toronto: C.D. Howe Institute.

———. 1997b. "Prudence and Performance: Managing the Proposed CPP Investment Board." Commentary 98. Toronto: C.D. Howe Institute.

Smetters, Kent. 1997. "Investing the Social Security Trust Fund in Equity: An Option Pricing Approach." Technical paper 1997-1. Washington, DC: Congressional Budget Office.

Social Investment Organization. 2002. "Talisman Signals It May Leave Sudan." Toronto: Social Investment Organization. http://www.socialinvestment.ca/News&Archives/news-601-Talisman.htm (accessed March 10, 2006).

Squirer, Lee Welling. 1912. *Old Age Dependency in the United States: A Complete Survey of the Pension Method*. New York: Macmillan.

Stock, James H., and David A. Wise. 1990a. "Pensions, the Option Value of Work, and Retirement." *Econometrica* 58(5): 1151–1180.

————. 1990b. "The Pension Inducement to Retire: An Option Value 36 Analysis." In *Issues in the Economics of Aging*, David A. Wise, ed. Chicago: University of Chicago Press, pp. 205–224.

Thane, Pat. 2000. *Old Age in English History: Past Experiences, Present Issues*. Oxford: Oxford University Press.

UK Department for Work and Pensions (DWP). 1998. *A New Contract for Welfare: Partnership in Pensions*. London: Department of Social Security.

————. 2000. *The Changing Welfare State—Pensioner Incomes*. London: Department of Social Security.

————. 2002a. *Simplicity, Security, and Choice: Working and Saving for Retirement*. London: Department of Social Security.

————. 2002b.*The Pension Credit: Long-Term Projections*. London: Department of Social Security. http://www.dwp.gov.uk/publications/dwp/2002/pencred/pencred.pdf (accessed August 23, 2006).

————. 2003a. *The Pension Credit: The Government's Proposal*. London: Department of Social Security.

————. 2003b. *Second Tier Pension Provision 1978-79 to 2000-01*. London: Department of Social Security.

UK Government Actuary. 2003. *Government Actuary's Quinquennial Review of the National Insurance Fund as at April 2000*. Norwich: Stationery Office.

UK Office for National Statistics. 2005. ONS Labour Force Survey. http://www.statistics.gov.uk/STATBASE/Source.asp?vlnk=358 (accessed August 23, 2006).

UK Pensions Commission. 2004. *Pensions: Challenges and Choices: The First Report of the Pension Commission*. Norwich: Stationery Office.

————. 2005. *A New Pension Settlement for the Twenty-First Century: The Second Report of the Pensions Commission*. Norwich: Stationery Office.

U.S. 1994–1996 Advisory Council on Social Security. 1997. *Report of the 1994–1996 Advisory Council on Social Security*. Washington, DC: Social Security Administration.

U.S. Census Bureau. 1960. *Historical Statistics of the United States, Colonial Times to 1957*. Washington, DC: Government Printing Office.

U.S. Department of Labor. 2004. *Private Pension Plan Bulletin: Abstracts of 1999 Form 5500 Annual Reports*. Washington, DC: Employee Benefits Security Administration.

————. 2005. *Private Pension Plan Bulletin: Abstracts of 2000 Form 5500 Annual Reports*. Washington, DC: Employee Benefits Security Administration.

U.S. Office of Management and Budget. 2003. *Budget of the United States: Fiscal Year 2003*. Washington, DC: Budget System and Concepts.

————. 2005. *Budget of the United States: Fiscal Year 2005*. Washington, DC:

Budget System and Concepts.

U.S. Social Security Administration. 2004. *Performance and Accountability Report, Fiscal Year 2004*. Washington, DC: U.S. Government Printing Office.

———. 2006. *The 2006 Annual Report of the Board of Trustees of the Federal Old-Age and Survivors Insurance and the Disability Insurance Trust Funds*. Washington, DC: U.S. Government Printing Office.

U.S. Social Security Board. 1937. "Social Security In America: The Factual Background of the Social Security Act as Summarized from Staff Reports to the Committee on Economic Security." Social Security Board Publication no. 20. Washington, DC: U.S. Government Printing Office.

Watson Wyatt Worldwide. 2003. "Pension Plan Solvency: Weathering the Storm." Special Memorandum. http://www.watsonwyatt.com/canada-english/pubs/specialmemoranda/showarticle.asp?ArticleID=11787&pdfURL=pdf/sm03-11.pdf&articledate=9/2/2003&Component=Memorandum (accessed May 18, 2005).

———. 2004. "Is There a Crisis? Survey of CFOs on Pension Plan Perspectives, Strategies and Reactions." Memorandum. http://www.watsonwyatt.com/canada-english/pubs/memoranda/showarticle.asp?ArticleID=13204&articledate=6/28/2004&Component=Memorandum&pdfURL= (accessed March 10, 2006).

———. 2005a. "More Companies Froze, Terminated Pension Plans in 2004, Watson Wyatt Analysis Finds." News release. http://www.watsonwyatt.com/news/press.asp?ID=14793 (accessed March 10, 2006).

———. 2005b. "Canadian Companies Reviewing Their Pension Plan Strategies." News release. http://www.watsonwyatt.com/canada-english/news/press.asp?ID=13072 (accessed May 18, 2005).

Whiteford, Peter, and Kim Bond. 1999. "Income Support, Retirement Incomes, and the Living Standards of Older People: Trends and Comparisons." In *Policy Implications of the Ageing of Australia's Population*. Melbourne, Australia: Productivity Commission and the Melbourne Institute of Applied Economic and Social Research. http://www.pc.gov.au/research/confproc/ageing/index.html (accessed March 10, 2006).

Whiteford, Peter, and David Stanton. 2002. "Targeting, Adequacy and Incentives: Assessing the Australian System of Retirement Incomes." Paper prepared for the 9th International Research Seminar on Issues in Social Security, Seminar on Pension Reform, held in Sigtuna, Sweden, June 15–18.

Whitehouse, Edward. 1998. "Pension Reform in Britain." Social Protection Discussion paper 9810. Washington, DC: World Bank.

———. 2000. "Administrative Charges for Funded Pensions: An International Comparison and Assessment." Social Protection Discussion Paper 0016. Washington, DC: World Bank.

Whiteside, Noel. 2002. "Constructing the Public-Private Divide: Historical Perspectives and the Politics of Pension Reform." Working paper WP102. Oxford: Oxford Institute of Ageing.

Yamada, Atsuhiro. 2002. "The Evolving Retirement Income Package: Trends in Adequacy and Equality in Nine OECD Countries." OECD Labour Market and Social Policy Occasional Paper no. 63. Paris: Organisation for Economic Co-operation and Development.

Yohalem, Martha R. 1977. "Employee Benefit Plans, 1975." *Social Security Bulletin* 40(11): 19–28.

The Authors

Alicia H. Munnell is the director of the Center for Retirement Research at Boston College and the Peter F. Drucker Professor in Management Sciences at Boston College's Carroll School of Management. Previously, Munnell was a member of the President's Council of Economic Advisers (1995–1997) and assistant secretary of the Treasury for Economic Policy (1993–1995). She spent most of her professional career at the Federal Reserve Bank of Boston, where she became senior vice president and director of research in 1984. Munnell was also cofounder and first president of the National Academy of Social Insurance and is currently a member of the American Academy of Arts and Sciences, the Institute of Medicine, the National Academy of Public Administration, and the Pension Research Council at Wharton. She is a member of the Board of the Wheeling-Pittsburgh Steel Corporation, The Century Foundation, the National Bureau of Economic Research, and the Pension Rights Center. Professor Munnell earned a B.A. from Wellesley College, an M.A. from Boston University, and a Ph.D. from Harvard University.

Steven A. Sass is associate director for Research at the Center for Retirement Research at Boston College. He has written a history of the U.S. private pension institution, *The Promise of Private Pensions* (Harvard, 1997), and Center publications on topics such as the reform of national retirement income systems, the management of risk in retirement income programs, and the extension of working careers. Previously, Sass was an economist at the Federal Reserve Bank of Boston. There he coedited *Social Security Reform: Links to Saving, Investment, and Growth* (Federal Reserve Bank of Boston, 1997), created the *Regional Review*, the Bank's economics magazine for the educated lay public, and directed the Bank's economic history museum project. Sass earned a B.A. from the University of Delaware and a Ph.D. from The Johns Hopkins University.

Index

The italic letters *f, n, t,* and *b* following a page number indicate that the subject information of the heading is within a figure, note, table, or box respectively, on that page.

Railroad Retirement System, 5
Replacement rates
    attempts to stabilize, 136
    in Canadian retirement income
        system, 109
Replacement rates under U.S. Social
        Security, 129, 139
    along with employer-sponsored plans,
        50*t*
    average earners' retiring at age 65,
        2005 and 2030, 11, 12*t*
    for hypothetical workers, 2006,
        47–48, 47*t*
Retirement age
    average age of U.S. men, 1910–2004,
        60*f*
    impact of 401(k) plans on, 59
    so-called normal, 65*n*2
    Social Security change to, in 1983, 56
    See also Early retirement incentive
Retirement before 1900, 21
Retirement benefits costs, 140
    See also Shortfalls in retirement
        funding
Retirement income of individuals
    ineffectiveness in creating, by
        individuals in UK, 85
    reduction of, from administrative
        costs in United States, 131, 131*t*,
        132
    by source in Australia, 1969, 1986,
        1996, 94, 94*t*
    by source in United Kingdom, 1979,
        71*f*
    by source in United States, 1979, 71*f*
    by source in United States, 2004, 8*f*
Retirement income systems
    evaluation of equity risks, 5–7
    evolution after Second World War,
        21–42
    importance of size in planning, 92,
        103–105, 138–140
    See also Anglo-Saxon nations'
        retirement programs; National
        retirement income programs
Risks

Age Pension (Australia) as protection
        against investment risks, 100–101
    evaluating equity risks in retirement
        plans, 5–7
    faced by Canada Pension Plan (CPP),
        118–122
    impact on different age groups of
        equities in U.S. Social Security
        program, 4
    from investments in equities, 136, 141
    and returns of particular assets, 52*b*

Saving. *See* National saving
Scandal in United Kingdom individual
        retirement accounts, 86
Self-employed Social Security tax, 56
SERPS. *See* State Earnings
        Related Pension Scheme
Shortfalls in retirement funding
    automatic adjustment mechanism for,
        119
    for U.S. Social Security system,
        10–11, 11*t*, 60–64, 61*t*, 127, 129
    See also Solvency issues for
        employer-sponsored pension plans
Social insurance programs
    Australia's lack of, 92, 94
    in Canada, 107
    in Canada vs. Britain, 123
    emergence, 25, 26–27, 26*t*
    vs. employer defined-benefit plans,
        118
    importance in emerging national
        retirement income programs, 27
"Social investment" strategies
    in Canadian retirement income
        system, 116, 117
    concerns in United States about,
        137–138
"Socially responsible" investment policy
    for Canadian retirement income
        system, 121–122
Social Security Advisory Council (1994–
        1996) proposals, 2, 62–63, 127–
        128
Social Security Reform (1983), National

About the Institute

The W.E. Upjohn Institute for Employment Research is a nonprofit research organization devoted to finding and promoting solutions to employment-related problems at the national, state, and local levels. It is an activity of the W.E. Upjohn Unemployment Trustee Corporation, which was established in 1932 to administer a fund set aside by Dr. W.E. Upjohn, founder of The Upjohn Company, to seek ways to counteract the loss of employment income during economic downturns.

The Institute is funded largely by income from the W.E. Upjohn Unemployment Trust, supplemented by outside grants, contracts, and sales of publications. Activities of the Institute comprise the following elements: 1) a research program conducted by a resident staff of professional social scientists; 2) a competitive grant program, which expands and complements the internal research program by providing financial support to researchers outside the Institute; 3) a publications program, which provides the major vehicle for disseminating the research of staff and grantees, as well as other selected works in the field; and 4) an Employment Management Services division, which manages most of the publicly funded employment and training programs in the local area.

The broad objectives of the Institute's research, grant, and publication programs are to 1) promote scholarship and experimentation on issues of public and private employment and unemployment policy, and 2) make knowledge and scholarship relevant and useful to policymakers in their pursuit of solutions to employment and unemployment problems.

Current areas of concentration for these programs include causes, consequences, and measures to alleviate unemployment; social insurance and income maintenance programs; compensation; workforce quality; work arrangements; family labor issues; labor-management relations; and regional economic development and local labor markets.